bookworm's food

aaron vergara

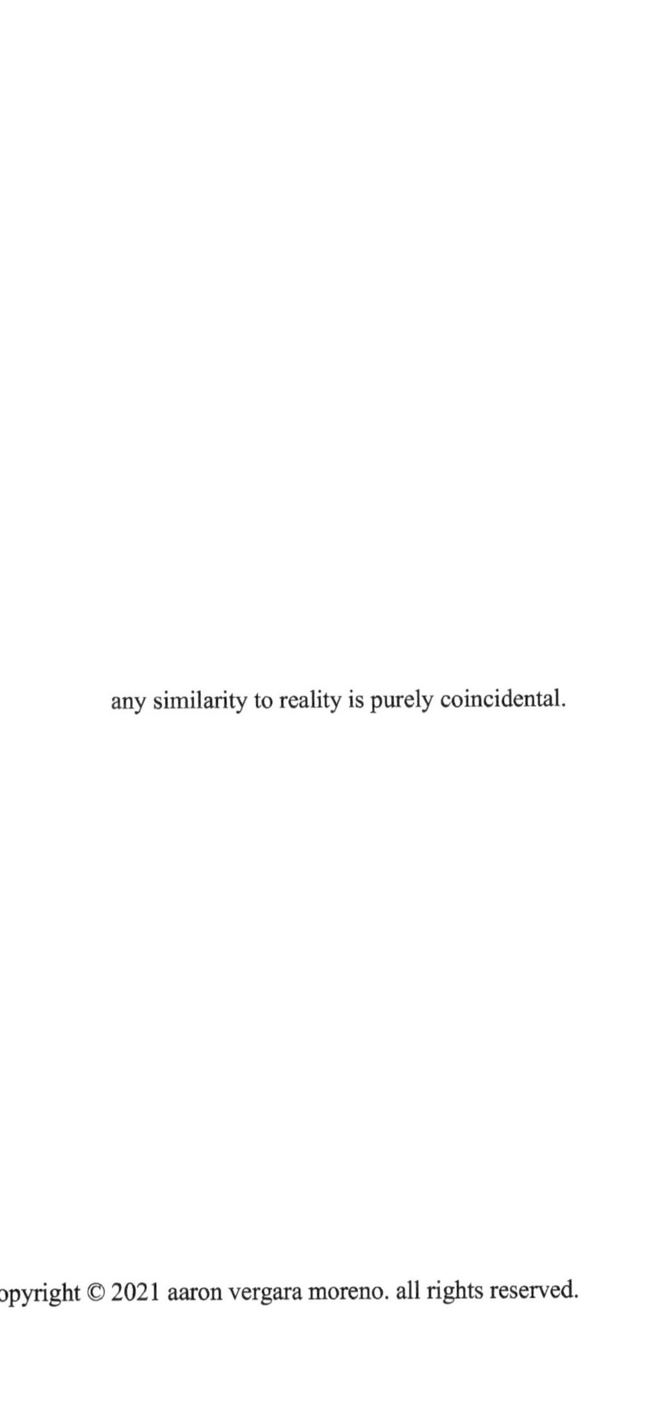

any similarity to reality is purely coincidental.

copyright © 2021 aaron vergara moreno. all rights reserved.

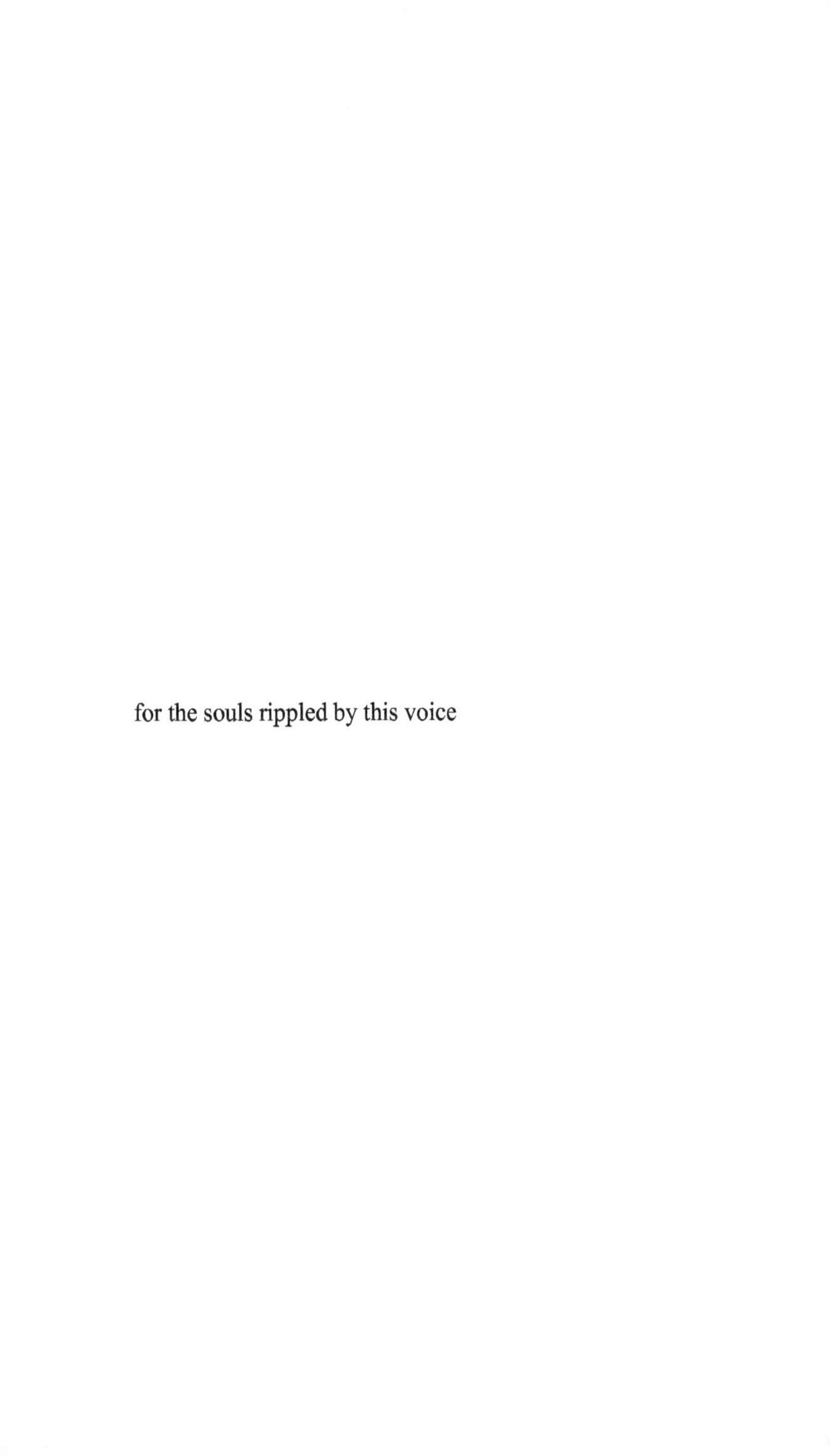

for the souls rippled by this voice

Contents

coexisting with a hazy state of mind

remembrance

father's day

we cooked and poured drinks for him.
we joked and tried to give him a nice day.
he told us that he cheated on my mother with three different women.
abruptly, i had three half-sisters
and sixty-five stabs in the back.

what makes family, blood, or bonds?

duoyun: books above the clouds

at the country's highest bookstore, one deciphers:
books are reflections—

you only see in them what dwells inside you.
you only resonate with the words that echo deep inside your fondness.

1999

the month is july,
you feel raindrops on the hair.
it is getting late.
it will be dark soon.
your mom calls you home.
with a warm shower, hot chocolate, and tv,
everything is fine.
is it possible to return to 1999?

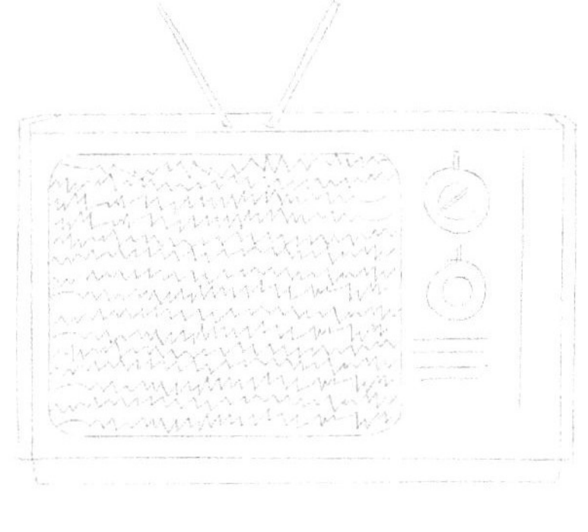

looks fool

a shy little boy with
his soft voice and
short stature

on the stage,
i opened
my mouth.
the audience
peeled open
their eyes.

my roar shook
the walls of an
auditorium.

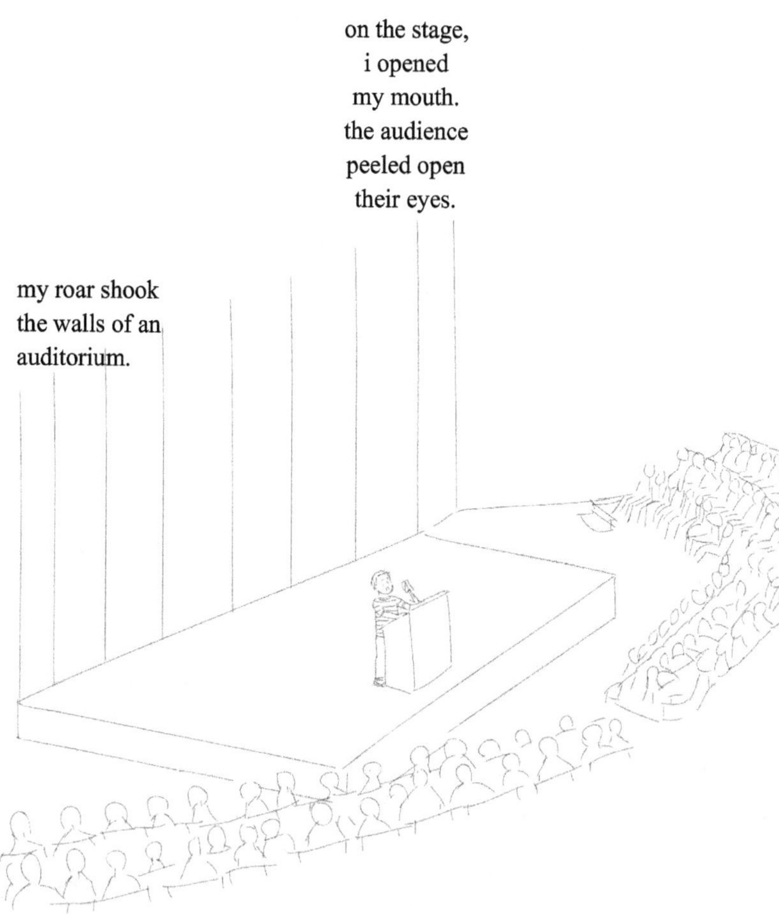

childhood

i had a very beautiful childhood
because i had luck.
i got to go to amusements parks
because i was a good son.
i got to visit the aquarium
because i won contests.
i got to see giraffes on a safari
because i competed in front of hundreds of strangers.
i got the latest video game
because i puked my food before my performance.
i got a big birthday cake
because i trained under hits and screams at 2:00 am.
victory was the way to access my lovely infancy
but it sowed atelophobia inside of me.
the people closest to us can damage us permanently.
isn't that right, mom?

low-income

poverty is bearable because food
is extraordinary.

we, the poor, society's discarded,
remember not to abdicate.

we overcome challenges,
with a bite of a humble bread.

prosperity to us
is getting to the point
where we never miss a meal.

luxury to us is the access
to succulent dinners.

food is our dream and relief.

memo to my child self

you wanted to be rich.
envious of other kids,
and the things they had,
you slept on a thin mattress on the floor—
you were poor
the entire family slept in a tiny room.

our simple-minded wishes
dreamt of liberty
in its most coercive form.
money grants freedom
in the form of a longer leash.

66,000

once a week, i used to sneak out from home to visit mr. v.;
he was nice to me and had his friends come over to chill.
they gave me candy and sips of beer, which mrs. o.
did not particularly like.
when i grow up, i want to be like mr. v.—
friendly, relaxed and full of candy, i thought.
on my last visit, i asked him about mrs o.
he told me she was already in bed, but she wasn't.
i searched all over the house.
on the roof, i found her sleeping
in an empty 2000-gallon water tank,
stiff and surrounded by mice.
i ran like a cheetah. i didn't know why,
but something in my tummy told me
my body was in danger.
what went wrong?
are all nice people like mr. v?
will i grow up a killer like him?
what did his parents teach him?
what will he teach to his two-year-old son?
is it possible to teach values one never learned?

raising a boy is a matter of life and death;
the boy, ripening into something other than a man.

that thing, whatever it became, will join an echelon of outlaws
yearly slaughtering more than sixty-six thousand beautiful
female hearts, thus increasing the staggering number of
unpunished

femicides

nel blu dipinto di blu

as a kid, i was influenced by cartoons.
i thought that in venice people were always singing
and moving around in gondolas.
during my first visit to the city,
i wanted so badly for reality to
match my childhood expectations.
i wasn't disappointed.
what a nice memory.

almost orphan

when she had cancer,
she hid it from me.
i wonder why?

it must have been
an impossible conversation
to tell your kid that you might die.

unexperienced

we were so innocent
and it was beautiful.
we were so naive
and it was horrific.

dad

any occasion she was crying,
i stared at him with enmity.

"do you know why is she like this?" i asked.

he couldn't sleep those nights; neither could i.

confusion was creeping on me.
i almost swung my fist

towards
someone
i thought was there to protect us,

towards
someone
i was there to protect.

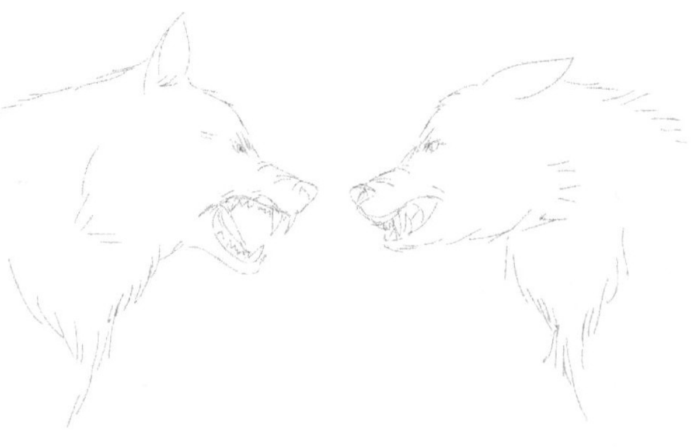

brother

i am cautious not to make a mistake.

there are few people that can bring my rage.

he is one of them.

i don't want to break or we will end up in a fighting cage.

just do not tell me what to do and do the opposite.

no one messes with my family

the punches of five bodyguards
punished me for hurting a bouncer.

the poor guy was so injured,
security called the police.

the policeman let me go
once i answered his question.

what did he do?

"he hit my older brother."

the way you molded me

all of a sudden,
guilt moved you.
you became the nicest person,
then expected me to change.

why do you feel sorry for the past?

your remorse can't reverse time.
i'm the result of your actions.
i do not resent you.
i'm just me.

alzheimer

we pretend nothing happened.
we prefer better times,
merry days, though we
didn't appreciate them then.

we know it can't be as before,
yet here i am, comfortably
living this fantasy
with a countdown to termination.

maybe memory loss is a way to find peace

also love, friendship and many more

human life is such an antinatural construct that to truly experience it,
one has to forget much of what one learned while growing up.

early days of covid-19

i've been so long on the run.
yet sedentarism has caught up with me.
the place i called awhile home,
feels like a prison i want to escape from.

where do i belong?

dude that writes

i ignore if i'm a poet or a joke.
no matter what i am, there are people out there
that share the same emotions,
people that these words will resonate with.
to all of you, this is my way of connecting with you.
i need you to convince me
that i'm not alone in this charade of a world.

ordinary life

we pursue normality despite the stories rotting our sanity.

fruits

together we shall rejoice
    during
        autumn,
           winter,
              spring,
               and
                 summer.
                   take a bite to crush my seeds with your teeth,
                     my fragrance will perfume your soul,
                 and your existence will turn endlessly delicious.

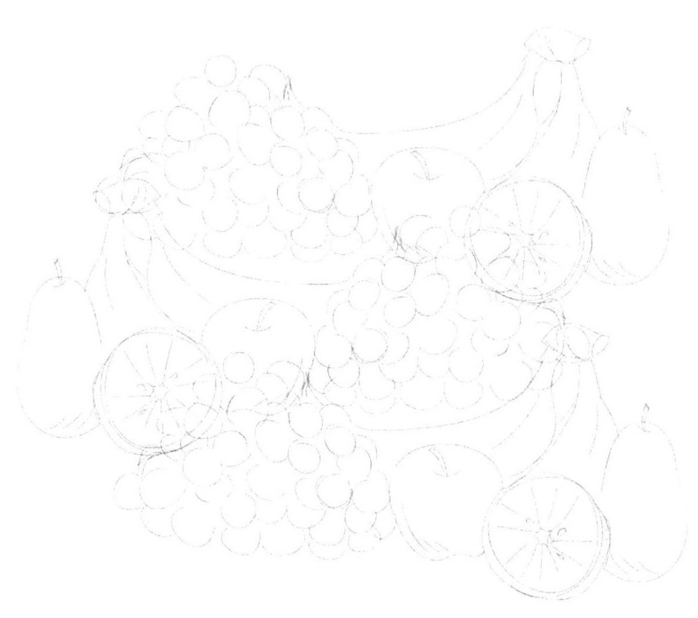

b-flat major

mozart composed a canon named "kiss my ass!" and i think that's beautiful.

corporate interview

boss: *so, can you cook tacos?*
me: have you tried, pastor?
boss: *hired*
me: …

principles of business

learn to compete
fierce feuds await.
we need team efforts.
talent will win us battles,
hard work, wars.

holiday

today is one of those days,
no alarm clock,
a gentle touch
of sunlight
wakes me up.

today, zesty tea,
playlists to dance,

i move on the streets
with a big fat smile.

strangers seem interesting,
my boss charming,
my teacher lenient,
my crush receptive.

today my friends are funny,
dinner is full of carbs.

the night aglow with stars
lightens my sleep.

my bed feels like a hug.

today feels like me on a good day.

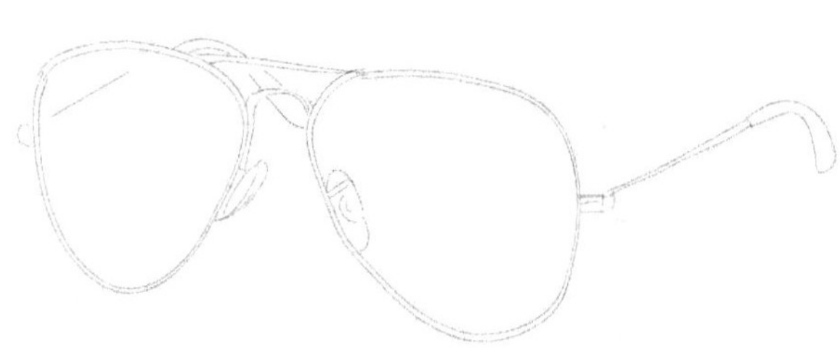

business consulting 101

competition is the worst.
creativity leads to places
no one else is profiting from.
monopoly is what we prefer,
a <u>blue ocean</u> for us.

introduction to business ironies

<u>perfect competitors</u> will claim they are unique,
monopolies will try to convince they are not.
deceive and deny,
their essence they hide.
it doesn't surprise the hypocrisy
behind their mask.
after all, businesses are run by people.

advanced corporate business

our oil rotted the soil, polluted the water,
sickened your infants with cancer.
if we pay, our business goes to hell.
we spend a fortune to avoid our crimes,
you die, our shareholders get a dime.
we create jobs and keep families safe
as long as you pay our bills with grief,
with children's corpses.

tailor-made lie

a well-dressed
pariah

purports to represent
virtue

and people
believe it.

shallowness reads
beyond any lexeme.

clothing is a perfect example
of a lie told without words.

sincere bs

he said bagpipes originated in scotland.
she said the moon has a dark side.
they said alcohol keeps you warm.
you say you are unparalleled.

it isn't easy to hear this deceit
from lying mouths
whose owners intend
to tell nothing but the truth.

i ignore what the truth is,
but i have become an expert
at unmasking what it isn't,
at detecting these sincere lies.

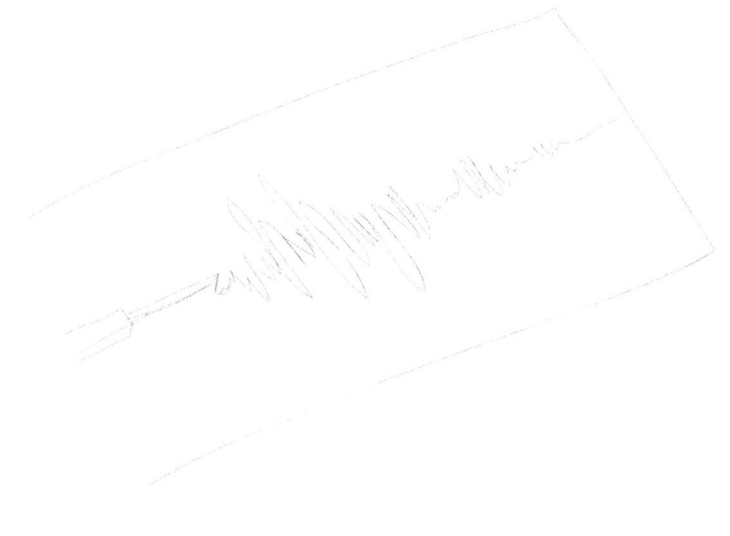

politically incorrect honesty

you heard me right; i mean everything i say.
i lit a fire bigger than your ego
just to look
at it,
just to see that your fragile soul can be swallowed,
just to watch you burn,
to observe your arrogance in ashes,
your pretense destroyed.

it is kinda fun

i find a special kind of fun
in letting people form an entirely
mistaken concept of me.

> only to then
> shatter their judgments
> piece by piece.

i find a special kind of fun
in letting people talk so sure
about things they're ignorant of.

> only to then
> subtly break their convictions
> and beliefs.

i find a special kind of fun
in toying with narrow minds.

bullies

a red masterpiece on a shirt—
for all i know,
it could be sold as a pollock.

the crimson pigments
came from the blood
of a rich punk.

his nose met my elbow,
a broken bone, and
art was born.

he shouldn't have attacked a defenseless boy

bullies trigger my rage.

ad verecundiam society

the genesis of our actions is rooted in the ideas of men from far-off eras.
the freedom of thought you are certainly proud of
is limited to the inherited work of the dead.
not many welcome unfamiliar perspectives, implying a contempt to be ruled

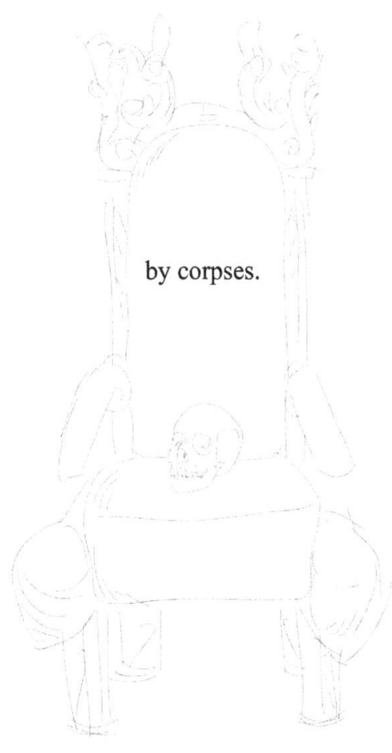

university

i arrived at this place full of kids pretending to know everything and knowing shit, ignoring how the world actually works. i saw no other option but to pretend to be one of them: a kid, one with several addictions. i won't lie, it was fun from time to time. we threw stuff from the seventh-floor balconies and ran around naked and wild. yet i knew i didn't belong.

could you please shut up?

people i detest:

hypocrites,

grumblers,

and people with dunning-kruger.

frat senryu

we gossiped at dusk:
laughs below the ashen sky,
mean jokes for dinner.

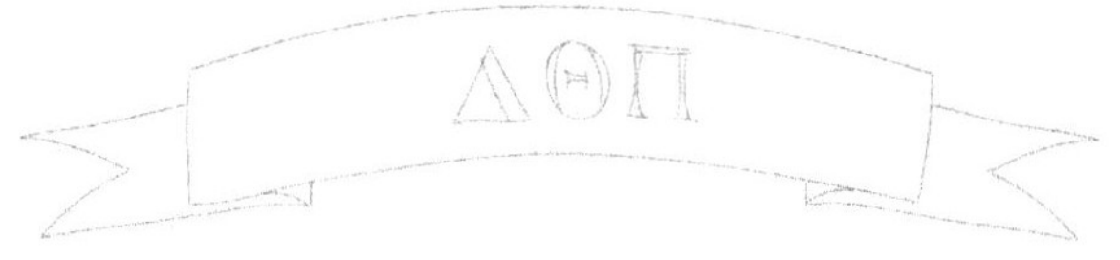

bubble

what can you possibly teach me?
i've been sixty years on this earth.

when you get to my age you'll get it;
i'm more experienced than you.

his earth is the agglomeration
of traditions and prejudices
from his small culture.

he never goes out of comfort
and the complexity of living
is reduced to a fraction.

he's convinced
of the completeness
of his incompleteness.

his earth
is a bubble

i'm sure

what determines the level of experience, time, or life?

some convictions we hold are already obsolete;
most will vanish through the immense span of time.
every thought will be surpassed
and likely seem ridiculous in 2000 years.

do what you can't!
no one truly knows anything.

meme conversations

anything you say may be used against you in a court of law, he said.

"boobies," i screamed.

she said, *what cologne are you using because i smell guilt.*

"damn, she is good," i thought.

you are proficient in disaster management, but here there's no catastrophe,

she said.

"you're welcome,"

 i said.

*chuckles.

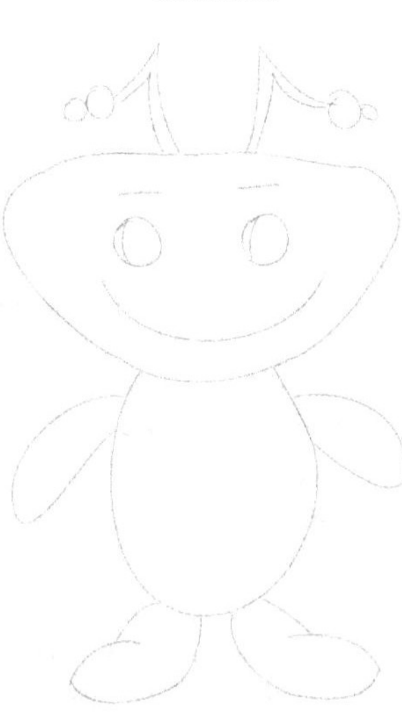

urban universe

you see, we loved big cities
and the wonderful feeling
of finding treasure in
every corner.

there are many countries in a cosmopolis;
depending on who explores the metropolis,
one discovers a multitude of
parallel worlds
within the same
physical realm.

never bored,
always new corners and subcultures
to explore

jorge

was the name i used to go by
to show a different persona
from mine from time to time.

he did heaps of jokes and pretended
to work uncommon jobs.
in conversation, he said he was once a hand model,
an aerialist, then a musician, and a stunt racer,
or whichever other job he invented on the spot.

was the alter ego my subconscious subtly telling me

that

i didn't like the person i really was?

nah,

i just did it for the "lols."

good ol' party

the chinese proverb 酒逢知己千杯少 translates to:
"a thousand cups of wine do not suffice when friends meet."
halfway through my hangover, i realized it wasn't about parties
but about people, those who made our time an incredible experience.
whether it was short or long, the time we crossed paths,
i cherish those moments and hope life gives me the chance
to meet you again.
until then, i wish you, beautiful party people,
to be real, be yourself, be true, but above all, be happy.

the squawk of chin chin and a melody of laughs,
i yearn for the tap dance of human decadence.
yes, i can't wait to move at the compass of our "decadance."

sex with the city

my beloved city
i love when we are alone in the dark.
you strip the prejudice away,
you undress my essence,
you reveal the lionheart,
and the mastermind.

dine and dash

i was sitting with j.
we were surrounded
by three bodyguards waiting for s.

he went for the money
to pay for a luxurious night.
he said he was paying,
though we didn't know how.

you see,
he whispered in our ears,
let's go for a smoke, outside he yelled,
run!

the bodyguards were faster
than our taxi.
the guns intimidated
more than our apologies.

the many hours we spent laughing
about how close we came to pulling that off
in a very dangerous place,

turned j. and s.
into my dearest friends.

—would he earn my respect? appreciation? gratitude? can i earn that? can i trust her? can i be certain? will he be a spiritless shadow? will she possess a dashing personality? will i be good for them or would i be a crack on the head? would i miss them, forget them? how can we build a friendship?[1] how would it be? brief? long? why do i ask all of these questions? is it my loneliness? boredom? curiosity? who is she anyways? who is he not? what do you eat? like? read? do? why are you here? how old are you? what do you want to achieve? what do you know? what do you ignore? would we get along? learn? grow? move on? — "jeez" so many questions, and only one that digs the answers: hey ... do you wanna get some drinks, do something stupid and laugh out loud?

---

[1] unwavering connection

overflowed

you will not be able to tell the precise moment when our friendship is formed.
as in filling a vessel drop by drop,
one last drop is what will make it run over;
so, in a series of moments, there is, at last,
one which makes affection towards others run over.

dear reader, may one moment in these pages
may one of my words, be that final drip.

teammate

whatever you are enduring,

you are not alone.

keep going,

i believe in you.

mole

she asked me
to describe
what it is to be
mexican.

only two words
to describe a
heterogenous race:

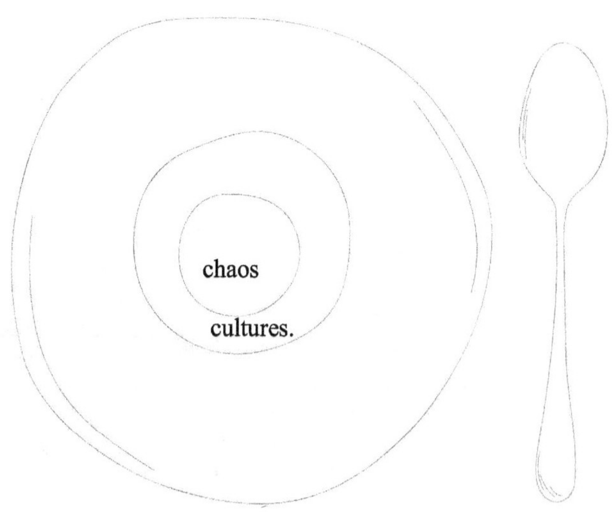

grassy afternoon

the smoky aroma of the grill,
good friends around,
drinks, smiles,
a big bite in a hamburger,
sun, cozy garden, and serenity.

beautiful.

salty afternoon

the soft breeze of the sea,
a relative to bond with,
pictures, anecdotes,
a liter of cold mango juice,
sand, radiant sunset, calm.

beautiful.

amber afternoon

the auburn color of the park,
a colleague to converse,
coffee, gossip,
a taste of pumpkin pie,
wind, empty walkway, tranquility.

beautiful.

white afternoon

the crackling chimney fire,
a lover to cuddle,
movies, caresses,
a gentle sip of hot cocoa,
snow, big window, harmony.

beautiful.

optimism

keep spinning the fortune wheel.
i'll keep watching
solely for my own amusement,
not to praise your luck
but to support you the moment
you discover it doesn't last forever.

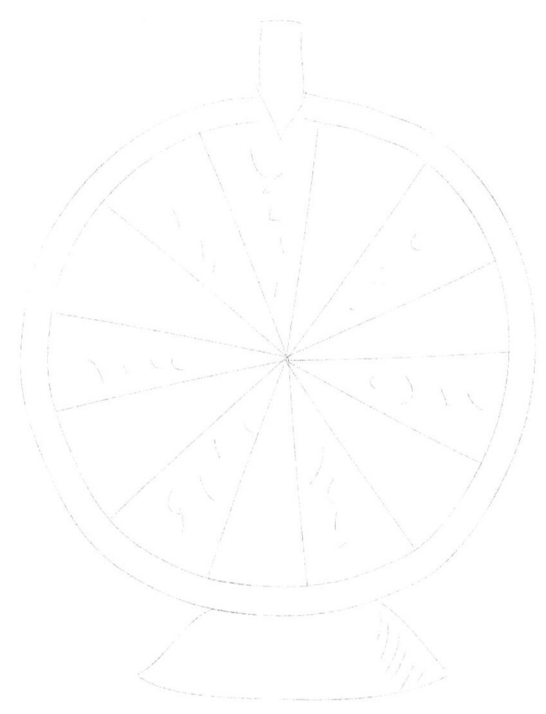

lights off – 14.03.20

i felt the hit, even though it wasn't for me, in the way something has to be,
the disorder, or the marvel, or the whole, something, anyway,
my cities on a break will soon reveal once again in the night
their safeguarding lights
that belong to me because i belong to them.

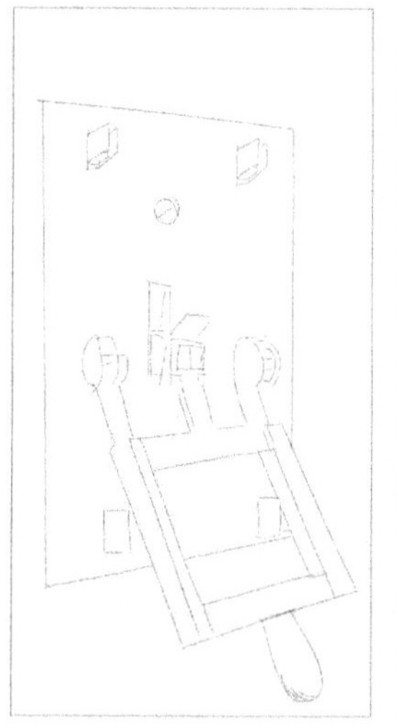 

hangover

i thought it was wise
to drown my anger
in moonshine.

that night,
i hurt a teen
with my fists

and

my beloved family
with my screams.

i can't recall details,
but my heart has a way
to make me remember.

don't let it happen again!

the night is old and sordid

uncountable terrors have been crafted under its veil.
piles of dreams have been promised by its magic.
the night has blessed romances for generations.
it has cursed stories over the eons.
the night being young is a fallacy.

places we avoid

society's anguish is forced to hide
and has its claws grappled onto the subworlds that we all deny.
drugs, human trafficking, theft, violence, murder, and many other dark acts
are the manifestation of our suppressed pain.
we are in deep sorrow and choose to look the other way.

social media

short, short stories i watch on a diminutive screen.
long, long have i bewailed the content of those stories.
for the very stress of finding a glimpse of sense, i am fain.

sociological objectivation

what's that dream that others have forced upon you?

what does your heart truly desire?

white void

you can revamp what besets the canvas.
    you can mend what is scrapped.
you can clean what dirties the palette.
    you can brighten a dark void.
but you can't fix what's not there.
    you can't fix a blank portrait.
you can't fix nothingness.
    you can't live in a white void.

worn-out

10,000 hours of effort, many more of desire.
training, practice, and zero mistakes.
i received pieces of advice and i gave all of myself.

i lost.

city dream.

Ambushed by sleep paralysis, I felt that horrifying caress produced by a demonic gaze. I was tied up by an obscure thirst, completely sweaty and aghast. I freed myself from the straitjacket, took a deep breath, fainted thinking everything was over. My dreams had other plans.

I had a conversation with old men, at the heights of the planet near the starry sky, temporality, and tangibility had no space. They asked, *"Naive teen, what is important to create?"* In the background,
there was an un-shun-able opposing scream.

I felt one hand on my ankle and tumbled in utter bafflement. A hoard of corpses dragged me, the rotten soil washing my clothes, yet their chant melodic as terrifying fighting against a sharpened yell.

"Existence doesn't admit outsiders, shatter your bubble, swing away from the sweet domesticating libretto of culture, feed your nothingness. Human simplicity is rather complex. Ask, learn, seek, grow, live,
let the permutations reveal your delightful uniqueness.

Life precedes essence, determinism is flawed, no rules, no laws, free, condemned with responsibility, alone without excuses. Unite your will with power."
Cadavers sang at the same time, an antagonistic sound urged me to ignore it all.

The words of the dead resonated beyond the uncountable speeches of the living. I let the ghosts bury my body under the mud as I heard the last order of the scary lifelong commanding screech.
Follow the recipe, a bulletproof script, stay safe, be okay, comply, obey.

In a matter of milliseconds, I felt a lightning bolt striking me,
high voltage electricity coming into my gut.
I rose from that nightmare and witnessed my voice's birth.
Never, I roared.

memo to my younger self

nothing is how you grew up believing it to be.
you'll soon enter a confusing world of disillusion, addiction, and void.
dark thoughts that you never imagined could exist
will scream at you in plain daylight.
infestation of worries that, hear it well, we'll never have again.

covid-19 ennui

i do not overthink about the future.
what is for me comes soon enough.

in the last 183 days, it has been different.
time, stopped; a virus advanced.

for a bit, this year felt like
many lost.

especially since i was recently made aware
that i have, at the very best, only a few more.

who knows,
maybe no more than the current.

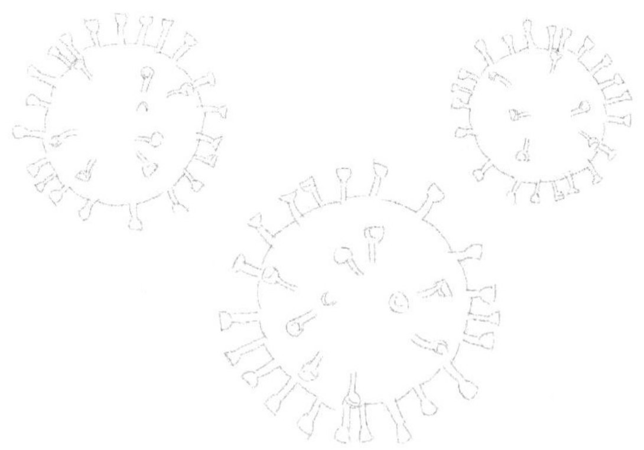

poet's routine

mornings

i put one foot outside my bed and encounter a geyser of doubts about myself.

afternoons

i attempt to find answers to my dreams and fears.

evenings

i go to bed at the foot of a volcano of thoughts
                          portrayed by my black-inked words.

bookstore stories

at the gates of the bookstore, one can read:
"the prelude is over, the main plot is about to start."

insomnia

humans swing between two taboos.

sex & death

both are still seen with guilt,
still discussed with caution,
still the origin of motion.

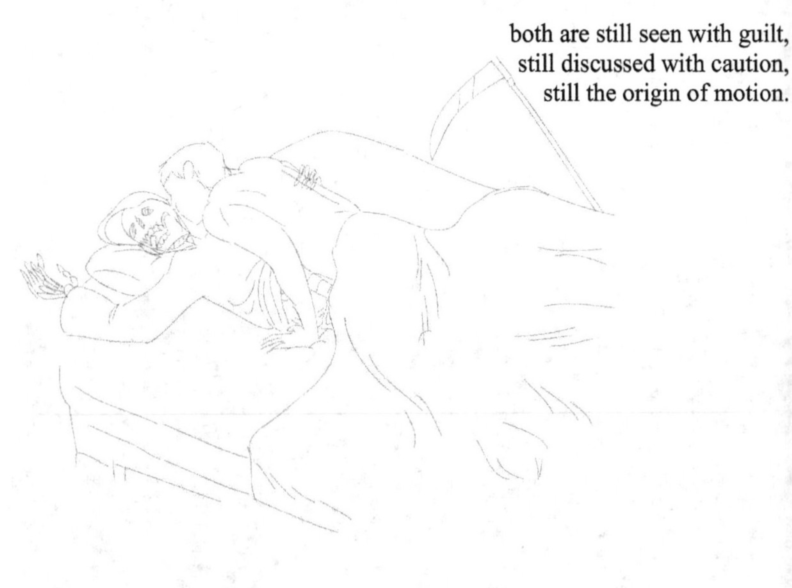

"mi cielo, sex is the consolation when you can't have love,"
is what you told me in bed.
if only i had taken your offer,
if I had decided to love you,
you wouldn't have run to him, and he
wouldn't have murdered you.
today, one year has passed, but you'll always be remembered.

rip,

my green-eyed sweetheart

reminiscence of unfairness

she would've been a personage;
the world would've known her face
until he ensnared her, exploited her,
dissolved her flesh with acid
in a street near her apartment.

and he became popular,
and she became one more name
of the girls murdered by him.
netflix made a series about him
and his atrocities.
and her mother
brought flowers to her grave.
and the priest
led a short prayer
in memory of her.

and i'm here wondering
if i'll ever meet another
splendid spirit like yours,
most likely not.

nice to meet you,

come near and you'll feel warmth,
but if you come closer,
make sure you are fire like me
or you'll burn.

malevolent kisses

she says *don't come looking for friendship or love;*
i'll shred your heart into dust.
she doesn't know
i'm turned on
by loves

      cooked by demons,

            served in hell,

                  eaten by sinners.

explosive getaway

when you have a fire of such caliber, you can only think of one thing:
to extinguish it. she didn't. she looked at my eyes and poured gasoline.
i saw a heart cleansed by dark; she saw a skin purged by fire.

dormant

hello there.
we share a common trait:
    evil!
come find yours.

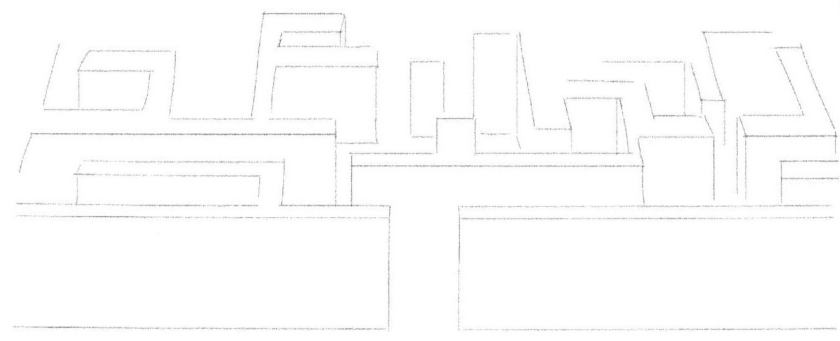

man-eater

she is an expert on men, toys with all of them.
she can make anyone cum and go.
she gets riches, attention and ejaculations;
claims to be the master of orgasms,
but she hasn't yet felt
one of the mind,
of the heart.

she began to love me

via noticing her longer conversations,
touching her smoother skin,
and tasting her warmer kisses,
looking at her livelier movements,
and smelling her intensified aroma,

her body told me to listen,
and i heard with all the senses of my body.

eating fears

i lifted the tip of her index finger with my left hand, the connection was palpable.
then, i grabbed her palm and combed her hair with my right hand.
my eyes looked at her tenderly while my mouth smiled subtly.
i pulled her head towards me, and she closed her eyelids;
after five seconds of savoring her lips, i got possessed.
i couldn't stop, i smooched her oral commissures, her neck, her shoulder blades.
i kissed her chest, breasts and abdomen.
i softly bit her back and massaged her spine up and down.
i ate her thighs, legs, and the cherry on the top of her sweet vagina.
i devoured her until her soul disconnected from her body three times in a row.
i did it once a day until she said – *i love you.*

sinful

i love you in a way that one loves what is forbidden;
between shadows and secrets

apology

for the man i could've been but wasn't.
to all my love stories,
there's one thing i've left to say.
i am sorry.

carolina

a straight haired-
brunette
with a short,
curvy, and trained physique,

                    she had an attitude,
            a soul made of fire, indeed.

the memory of her
turns me voracious.

            when repleted of chaos, isn't the body a delicacy?

C. C.

direct approach

the crowd was admiring her beauty and wealth.
she appeared to be a celebrity,
definitely not a woman from around here.
the crowd mumbled and
i heard *who is she?*

well, let's find out!

nervousness

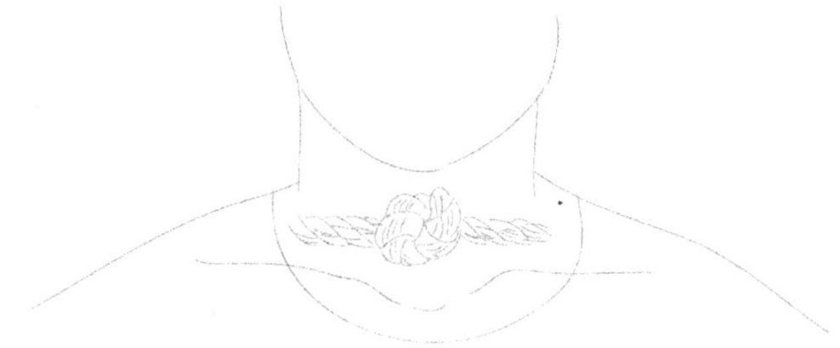

he has a crush on her,
trembles in their meetings
behaving nice and shy.
his chest is warm,
his heart beating hard;
there's a kind of power
pushing him back
from her heart.

first dates

i'd like to imagine that you enjoyed the brief moments.
that you opened the chat and started thinking of something to say...i do.

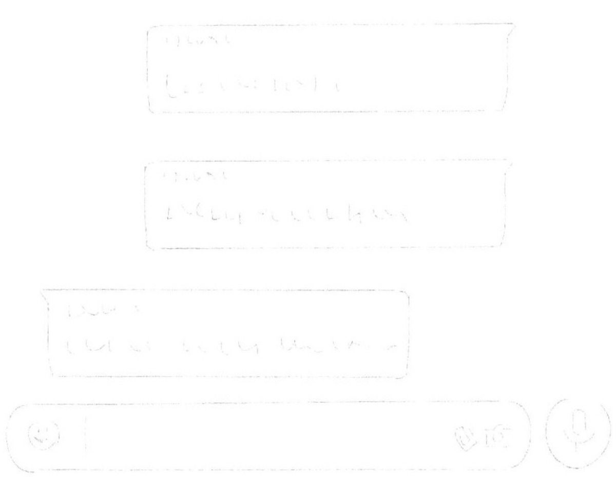

when i see her,

i don't give a darn about privacy; i'm an open book.
you only need pop the questions,
i won't sing by my own.

although, when i see her,
i'll be damned.
what a voracious hunger for
her reading the pages of my lips,
for telling her the truths behind my look.

and so, between pints and pints, certainties.
and so, between hookup and hookup, contradiction.

naked man

she saw through the clothes.
my soul was helpless and lost.
she was the first to see me naked.

disney educated

the sincerest teenager on the block missed several chances to grow. to gain the
sympathy of a pretty girl, he constantly jumped into an abyss without a plan b.

he loved anyone who just entered his confusing life.
what a fool was that ignorant juvenile with a noble heart.

sexy bad girl

she was draining my innocence

       and pouring something else into my head.

disorder of life

don't ask for permission, forget protocols.
enter the depths of my soul.
do not restrain from making a mess.
if we both suffer, time will repair us.
calm down, breathe deeply.
disarrange my life.
brace for chaos.

vulnerable

to the people we let enter our lives,
we are implicitly telling them:
you are allowed to hurt me
the bliss you bring
is worth the risk.

i still don't know what dazzled me more,
your exquisite silhouette in a vibrant blue dress
or the sound of gun shells as you shot an AK-12.
it's time to accept what life has for us.

too close, yet too late to fulfill an eleven-year promise
that lies shattered on the floor like our crystal rose.
blinded by emotions, we feared and made the most naive mistake—.

naive to ignore that promises
are not the way to keep something extremely blithe.
naive to notice that promises
are animal cages unknowingly used to dissect feelings.
naive to accept that promises
are a cowardly form of control.

it's happening again, you were wrong in many ways,
yet you were right in the most important way of all.
fuck this curse that you cast on me;
your voice still echoes in my most frightening dreams.

i see you lurking from time to time
in the present stories of my life.
i imagine you are
telling me to prove you wrong.
i want it too.
i'm trying.

one day i will find it;
one day our silence will receive an answer.
until never and merry marriage,

my slavic sun

O. I.

swiss ski

at 6:00 am, when we woke up, we were snowflakes.
at noon, we became a snowball, hail, blizzard.
at midnight we became an avalanche under the moonlight.

she's my shepherd

'cause when i'm down, i pray to your body.
'cause when i'm hurt, i go to you, my church.

walk the talk

she didn't understand the logic behind a rose:
just like people,
if you take care of them,
they'll blossom.
        my words were halfway there;
        i was just waiting for my deeds
        to sing to her ears.

zero promises

no! stop! don't promise me anything!
promise only to yourself, promise that you will always be happy,
and as long as i do my job bringing joy to your soul, i know you will take care.
i don't want you to stay because of something as cowardly as a promise.
i want you to stay because i'm still capable of make you love me.

promises meant to be broken

an ephemeral heart with an eternal promise—
i knew you were full of shit when you said always and never.
those words are too strong for weak human spirits.

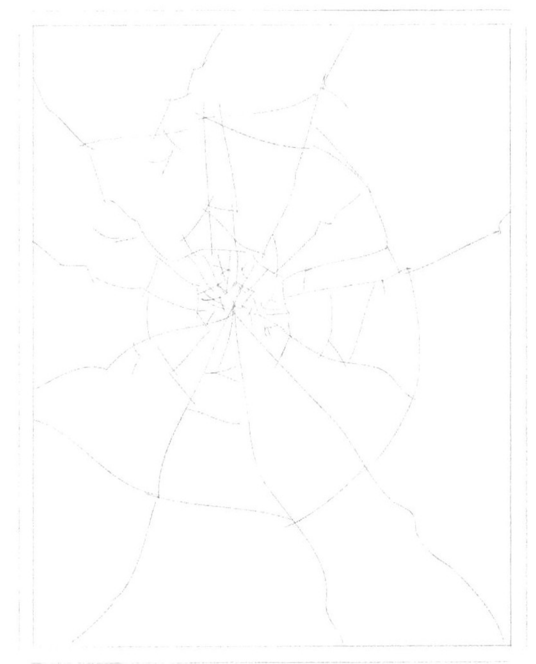

amateur convictions

you fight to prevent her from making a terrible choice

or

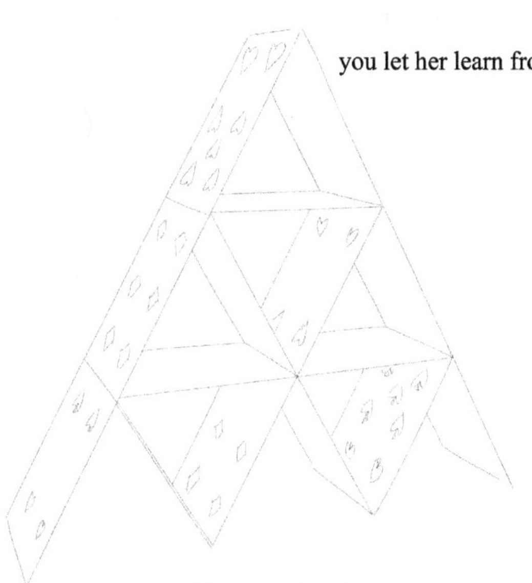

you let her learn from a big mistake.

either way, just be there,
no matter the outcome.

first and last time

she struggles saying hi.
he sweats at goodbye.
why are firsts and lasts hard?
is that why we prolong the latter

as much as we can?

made in new zealand

made of flames and tides,
of catastrophe and peace,
nature and city,
laughs, tears.
made of flesh,
of rights and wrongs,
cuddles, kisses, glass, steel.
made of
wild dreams,
spontaneous decisions,
goals and fear.
made of unquenchable will.
made of her universe.

R. P.

seasonal proximity

if i only could be the summer breeze
and lift your dress when
you aren't expecting it.
if i only could be the autumn wind
and touch your skin when
you aren't expecting it.

expiration date

i noticed the book in her purse;
she carried it everywhere
and reread it repeatedly.
i and my energic
curiosity couldn't resist.

what's
        inside?
it was the quintessential
story of
romance.

she was one of many girls
who are in love with ideas,
not people.

while breaking many hearts along the way,
she can't find what she's looking for
and is becoming one of many girls
who do not believe in love.

that's when i realized
she loved because she loved love.
sadly, she didn't love me.
we started a relationship with an expiration date.

and so, we infatuate our ideas,
        and so, we create our checklists,
and so, we reduce complexity to whims,
        and so, we never learn that
                loving is not shopping!

sincerity

you wish for love, laughter and happily ever after.
for the third, i'm not so cruel as to sell you lies.
it's not clear to you why, for my thoughts reflect shadows of feelings,
intrinsically dimmer, emptier, and simpler.
yet, i'll devote myself to you for the remaining days.
you'll begin to fathom one notion:
whatever is done for love always occurs beyond right and wrong.

origins

have you heard latino songs?
some are based on those who know that
love can't be forced, chosen, or conditioned;
we only reckon free and fierce.

        the song i dance to?
        inspire a girl to achieve bigger things
        while
            loving
                her
                precisely
                    the way
                        she is.

what bothers me?

we won't laugh at a silly meme.
the constant messages no longer arrive.
we won't count the days 'till we meet again.
plans will be dumped into a garbage can.
we won't share the little pleasures,
and your name will be written in the book of my failures.

we played with
karma
          and love.

jokes on us.
all
is gone.

warnings pointed
the drama to avoid.
fuck off.

find me in spaces full of
silence
          and words.

sorry for the scar;
i have one too,
a beautiful one.

goodbye,

my lively darling

M. K.

pet love

his love rises from the dream of what she could become,
but he sees her as a collection of imperfections,
and constantly tries to persuade her into behaving in a certain way.
he tries to mold her and turn her into an indoctrinated extension of himself,

i decided
to steal her love
from him.

train ride

once they step into the wagon,
they'll lose their ability for wonder, for not knowing.
it will occur and nothing in the universe will reverse it.
even at the point of return, they'll never truly leave.

home for the homeless

christmas is a beautiful paradox.
      we travel like nomads, homeless and joyful.
            darling, is this path leading to the roots of the festivity?

she told me "i love you"

what to do with words that have been heard in the past,

that have been heard in former stories.

big claims call for big proof.

anticipated farewell

my crazy darling,
truths we now discern.
we're far from each other, yet so close in mind,
next to one another, yet far from being what we want.

a risk, a mystery, and the most certain thing
that we have in our lives
we're continents apart, but our memories are as one,
fear that this goodbye could be the end
of this mad, ludicrous, and intense memoir.

the adage?

there are thousands of people one can be with,
                       but there are so few with whom one can truly **"be."**

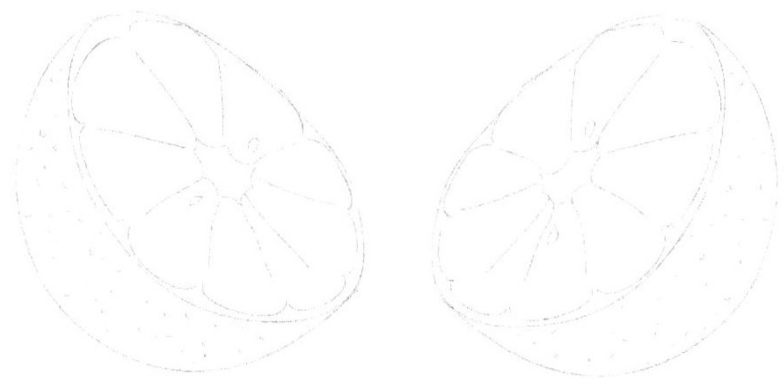

gone

you are getting what you wanted
a break, an escape from reality,
an experience of a lifetime,
a piece of my world.

but now you've decided
to suppress your hopes
for a present with me
to gamble them for
a future with him.

i warn you: once i walk away,
i'll stay gone.
you can't have it both ways.

separate ways

you'll be left alone with kiss marks all over your body
and buoyant moments in your memories.
the things that seemed impossible
now seem inevitable,

and

you no longer wonder
what it's like to be stranded
in a natural disaster.

six years ago, on a road trip, i grabbed your hand and said,
"c'mon, quick, let's run!" and run we did.
we fled our tent and ran towards the deserted beach.
we kissed among the fiery sea waves
and fornicated on the fine brown sand.
our witnesses? the heat, the night and the fullest moon
i've ever seen in my life.
it didn't feel fun; my overwhelmed senses made it clear
it was my very first time making love.

that's the secret, and you took my heart for many years,
and left a scar so large.
it's been a while, and i haven't heard from you.
it's been some time, and you haven't heard from me
and i hope it stays that way.

alles gute,

mi vida

feierabend:

when it reached the time of the day, in which i could see her smile,
all the work of the day gained meaning.

homo erethizontidae

> your hugs
> are the highlight
> of this unexciting week.

i'm fond of your hands
pressing against my back,
of your arms
pulling
my body
towards yours.

> i like the trust we build,
> getting closer, one hug at a time.

we bind until our quills
pierce through our bodies
and impale us
with razor-sharp pain.

> humans are porcupines,
> with quills hidden
> until we are too close.

and i want to hug you as twice as strong. should i?

high-yield investment

your smile blinds me from the world
and i try desperately to keep your lips upturned.
you could say my affection is shown
through my efforts to bring you joy

while my life fades away.

although, my appreciation
is not measured by
what i'm willing to do
but by what i'm willing to gamble
and lose for your happiness.
by doing so,
i sow death in me
to harvest bliss in you.

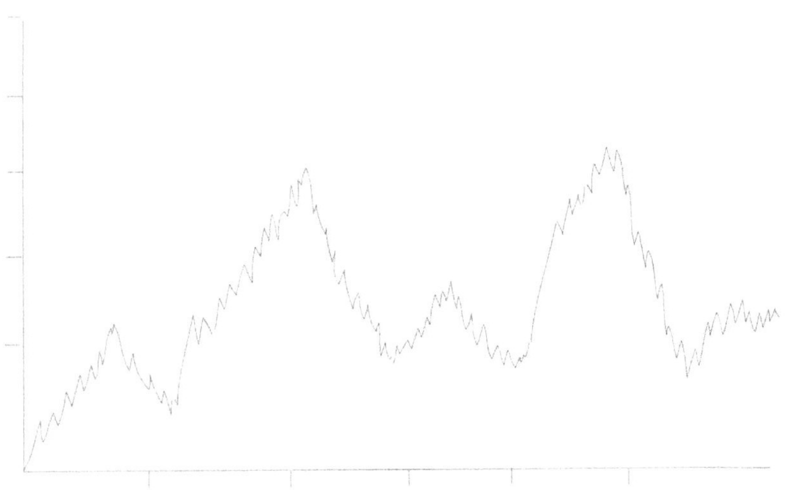

70 years

every night we lie in bed,
and i close my eyes;
a vision comes to me
through the fog,
through a door
that no one crossed before.
i dream of what our world could be:

70 years are keeping me awake.
70 years is all is going to take.
70 years to live in a dream we design.
70 years for the world we will create.
however big, however small ...

what's the price of love?

one full life.

i am dust after all

i'd love you, strong, honest, and pure.
i'd love you for long, 5, 10, 20, or 70 years.
i'd love you how it's meant to be,
but not forever.
my ephemeral body can't give eternity.

doves in the wind

during that time, marriage was all i thought about.
i naively believed i was getting married anytime soon.
right now, it seems to be the thing i will never experience.
with time, i learned that we don't settle down because of the right person.
we settle down because we are finally ready for it

                    with whatever person we are dating,
not necessarily the best one or the prettiest,
just the one who happened to be on hand when the time got to be right.

                  unromantic, but still true … such bullshit.

desperation

i didn't understand her anorexia nor her anxiety.
i never truly endured her visits to the therapists or the psychiatric clinics.
i didn't know how to handle darkness.
i should've known so many things.
i wasn't able to handle my demons,
how could i have handled hers?

mourn

i will never forget
how i felt when
i realized she was gone:
hollow, pointless and
swimming in a river
of tears and decay.

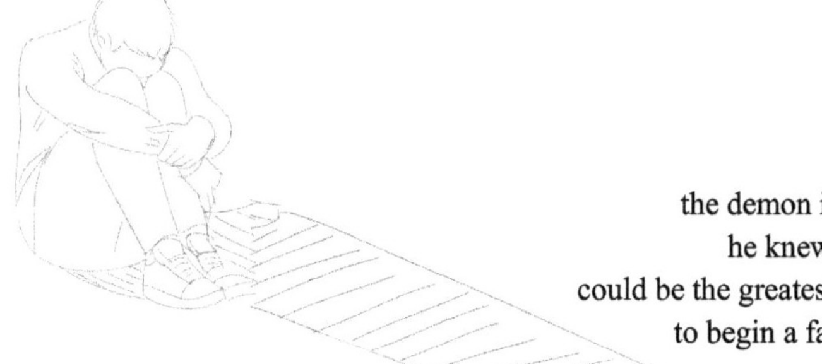

the demon in me smiled,
he knew that tragedy
could be the greatest opportunity
to begin a fantastic story.

together we learned what's to burn:
such passion, such fire,
so fast, so short,
sinful, lustful, wonderful.

you ate my distrust; i devoured your fears.
you painted a degas on my skin;
i wrote a hemingway with your moans.

we consumed each other badly.
we can't be in each other's lives.
we'll have to live in one another's art.

take care, farewell,

my ardent painter

K. S.

unfamiliar muse

to write, one needs inspiration
sometimes from a muse
who knows the elysian mystique
of closing the eyes,
uncontrollable laughs,
crying heartily,
tender kisses,
dreaming vividly,
consecutive orgasms.
the best things in life
exist beyond the landscape of our eyes.

we have more kids than men

a man can't be a man without a woman.
being a man is an acquired trait,
not one inherited at birth.

a man needs a woman
who knows how to
sculpt,

        who, with her chisels, forges
        the perfection
        of a male,

carves a perfect proportion
between
warrior and companion.

we need strong, solid men;
we need more women artists.

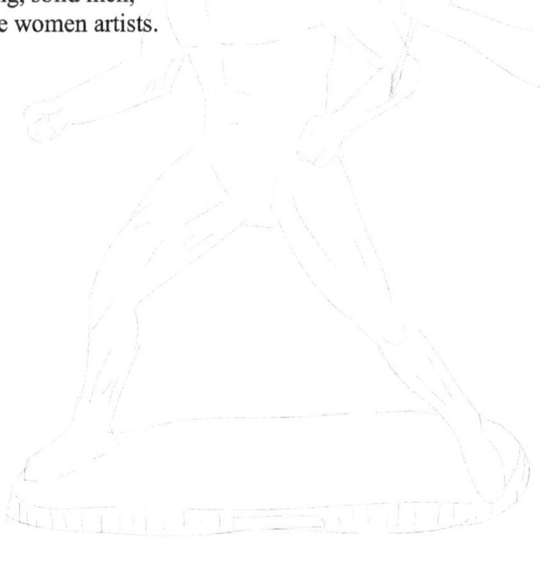

ballroom

feel the beat,
start slow,

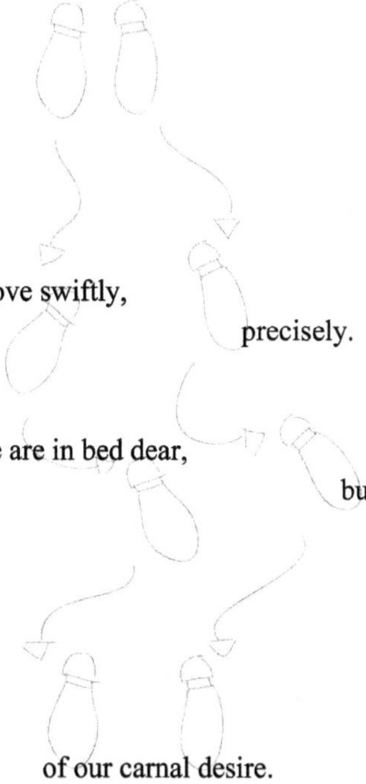

move swiftly,
precisely.

we are in bed dear,
but this is a dance

of our carnal desire.

bed & sheets

she asked him for music.
he intertwined his fingers with her palm creases,
used her thighs as earphones,
and he,
with his tongue,
made her sing.

sex is art

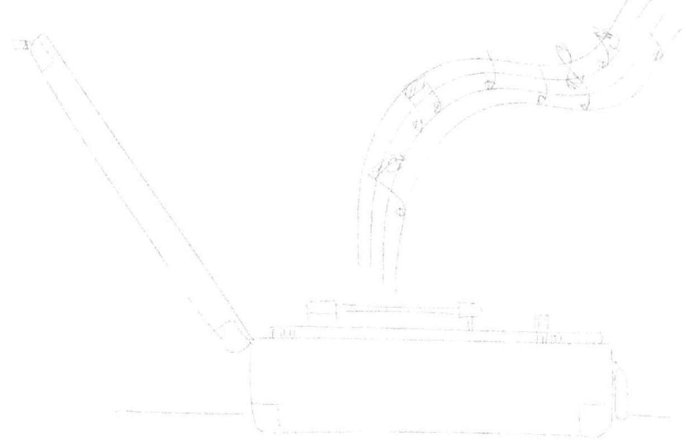

eyes

blue, green, brown, or black—what color eyes do you prefer?

white, rolling over and discharging sensual hunger.
white, as your shaky body close to climax empties its mind.
i fancy utterly honest,
       sheer white, while i snowboard the curves of your legs
                  one whole night.

passion

fuck hard, **love** strong.

bestial denial

bite me! scratch me!
my demands attempted
to bury with lust the evidence
that you were becoming
my flare during winter,
an ember that had to be
turned to ashes by the end of the season.

white light

Shortly thereafter, the wretchedness of my psyche, a burgeoning warmth surfaces on my chest. I quickly hypothesize bruises healing in my core metamorphosed into intriguing matter. Carefully rappelling downwards into the caves of my not anymore benighted gestalt, I behold a powerful enigmatic shine. Introspective diffraction unveils the colored wavelengths latent in my Love.

Ablaze with assailable lust from every bygone climax born on my skin, chisel continuous orgasms between thy legs until a paroxysm of exhilarating red kisses scintillates our bodies' rhapsodies.

Sink the erratic anguish of this mad world neath a nether sea of appeasing knowledge and humility. Purvey an intellectual pickaxe for thee to pry the alluring blue sapphire that thee are deep inside.

Perplexed by the abyss of thy singular persona, plunge into winsome chaos, hug fears, cauterize wounds, extol insecurities and shush noises, wallow the heart in a cyan watered coast of support.

Craft superb out of mundane, for god's sake, confined in a meager chamber, imagination ignites magic of violet agapanthuses exuding our reveries and chortles—an aroma the world misses out on.

Chaos bestowed a wide panache upon my spirit by variegated ordeals in the past, let it assemble consistency in the diminutive, innocuous things to hoist living at comfort zones upwards to green, prosperous fields.

Cosset health nourishes resilient spiritual states, clash words, close chasms between souls and cogitate in a sacred orange shrine exorcising mistakes and wars. A lasting dawn of peace springs.

Brawl any obstacle to grasp the enticing wrinkles on the lips, the ravishing curvature on the mouth, charioteer under a yellow twilight silhouetted against a gorgeous smile is to postpone one's demise.

This visible spectrum circulating in my veins provokes a catharsis to expand my sight. Strong feelings need no protection, they're fierce bulwarks. I shed my unconditional light on anyone's concealed grim cries. And yet, this bravery hesitates to end a perennial search for another's troubled eyes which also produce in the dark a radiant white light.

poet's crucifixion

how is it possible to relive all those trying moments?

you bleed

your thoughts if i say ...

when i write,
i hope to spark
the imagination
and recollection
of a reader,
and by doing it,
i can argue that
one word is worth
a thousand images.

... love?

uncommon

i am skeptical about loves
that exist as often as
a sunset and a sunrise.

i believe in loves
which are as common as
a solar eclipse.

years can pass without
hearing about them.

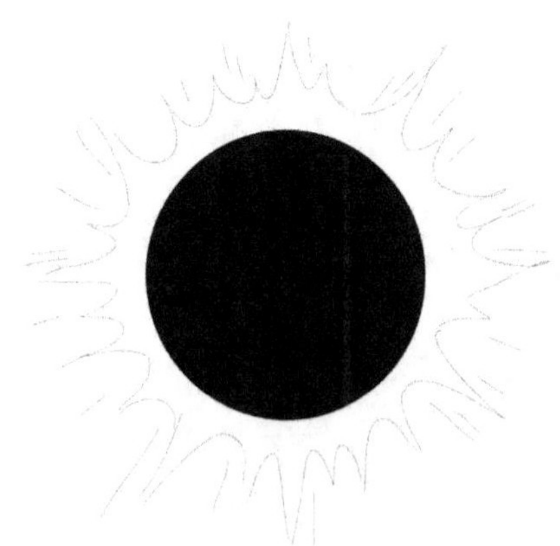

love stories

sweetie, wanna hear something inspirational and beautiful? say your name.

for sale: engagement ring, never worn.

congratulations, it's a girl!

horror stories

"good morning, love," he heard from the empty room.

"i am willing to do everything to make you happy,"
she said before he started strangling her.

"where are we going, honey?"
she said when he stopped to catch a breath
after hours of running away.

roads to rome

lisa decided to leave;
she stopped baring julie.
then, lisa's liver failed,
cancer came roughly.

julie was terrified
of being alone
at her age once again.

julie donated half liver.
lisa couldn't go away.

they became
a happy couple born
from fear and guilt.

silent killer

sarah was tired of matt.
sarah kissed him goodbye
on the neck
with a silver knife.

jacob professed his love for her;
mary said she would leave
jacob made her stay,
her cadaver can't walk away.

mia was drunk and infatuated,
james crashed the car.
mia & james didn't make it,
neither did little emily's family.

ignorant love kills silently.

what is love?

a life lesson.

inauguration of depression

today i felt odd,
out of place,
not evil or good.

where's the joy
and the pain?

i only find indifference.

is this how it feels to be broken?

i don't have a clue
about the reasons behind
this lack of strength to fight.

one tear reflects against clear blue sky;
is it a temptation to embrace pathos?

is it that i am lazy and unmotivated?
i can't even fathom what is wrong.

i don't think it will last long.
please don't.

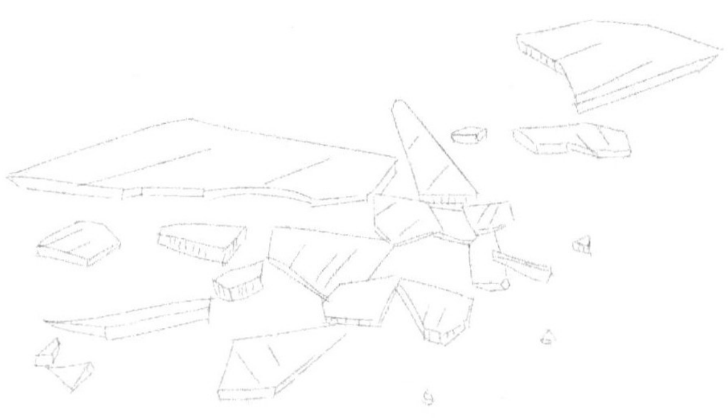

fill in the blanks

i did ____

and i ____

this ____

and this ____

made me ____

and omit ____

i was committed to being the worst version of myself.

lonesome

i went back home; it's been there all along.
i return to where i belong.
i'm back, did you miss me?
come now, give me one of your sweet kisses,
my perpetual solitude.

molly

arthur was my comrade,
dear friend, family
living inside the claws
of a great tragedy.

i didn't call, didn't visit,
didn't support him
in any way whatsoever.
why wasn't i there for him?
it is simple, i fell head over heels in love,
and she was the sweetest thing i'd ever known.
she made me feel all the warmth and happiness i had lost for a long time.

her name was mdma.

busy days

i'm busy now.
i'll call you tomorrow.

the day after, a nurse answered,
my colleague had liver failure.
he died at 09:00.
i didn't even know he was at the hospital.

now, i speak with kindness
and patience to anyone as if they'd die tomorrow.

not for him, not for you, not for anyone else;
i do it for the sake of our humanity.

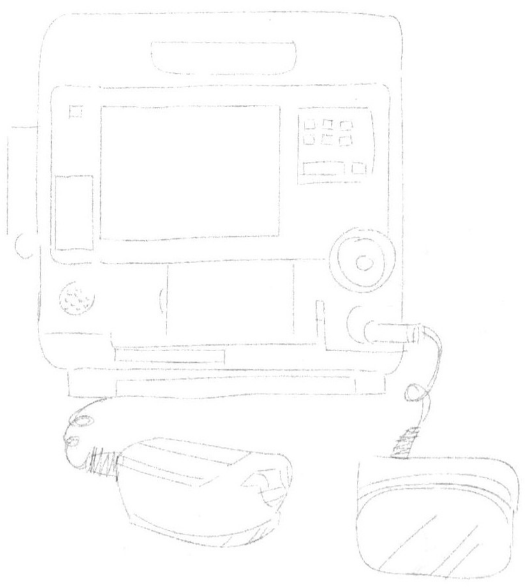

not boring weekend

phone calls have always made me anxious:

i was eating in a restaurant with isabel, a very close acquaintance of mine.
we were sitting and listening to a man with a heavy voice and an angry attitude.
the man told us hard-to-swallow stories that carry you onto a rollercoaster of
emotions. first, he told us that if everything went well, we would be relaxed, in
the comfort of our homes sipping on a cup of hot chocolate with marshmallows.
then, he told us that if i didn't share some details with him, he would murder
my family after shooting isabel. he somehow knew our address and phone
numbers. finally, he contacted my family, who happened to be on a trip outside
the city, and told my brother another story that if he didn't cooperate, i would
be beheaded later that day. this was not uncommon in the dangerous city where
i used to live. the man asked for an amount impossible to get for a working-
class family… i never saw the man; isabel and i just heard his voice over the
phone
while his gunmen were chaperoning us.

he found our number in the yellow pages

luckily, the kidnapper didn't find out about my beloved girlfriend, who i sent
to a safe place before isabel and i fell into a kidnap trap.
if he had used her as a bargaining chip, i would've wreaked havoc. i would
have been forced to turn a transaction into a bloodbath— i didn't know if i
would triumph or end up lying on the floor as a corpse.

holy protection

the victim believed in acts 18:10.

the criminal in jeremiah 29:11.

one day, at the end of its corrupt career,

the felon read romans 6:23,

prayed following philipians 4:6,

and got john 10:10.

the victims stopped believing in romans 8:28.

zero sum game

her extended shaky arm told me everything,
what is not her job,
what she does not think,
what she does not believe,
what she doesn't eat,
how much she doesn't weigh,
how much she doesn't have.
i only needed to know why the beggar kid was poor.
is it because her nakedness dresses me and her hunger feeds me?
i wish i could do more for her yet …

on a sunday,

i visited her grave and wondered
how her murderer could be that evil.
what is truly evil
is the power to murder someone,
and whoever holds that power is cursed;
no matter what,
no happiness could come from it.
humanity is cursed.

lurid bridge

i wake up in the mornings
with the terror of finding out
about your lifeless body
hanging from a bridge.

your murderer could be any
from the many
drug thugs
infesting this city.

any moment,
i could receive news
that would make me
drop to my knees.

that's life in this town
every fucking day.

how do i prepare myself to stare at your cold body hanging from a bridge?

serenity

it's easy to be driven by testosterone
and fight against the world,
but waiting and trusting
someone to return
when there's a high chance they won't?

that shit requires strength.

strifes

strifes got awfully grisly astonishingly swiftly
strifes got grisly shamefully instantly
really strifes got grisly improbably briskly
truly strifes got grisly clearly rarely
originally strifes got grisly ironically frequently
greatly delicately strifes got grisly unsuccessfully
sporadically strifes got grisly particularly painfully
silently seemingly strifes got grisly elegantly.

serious rapport

why do you run from meaningful conversations?
what are the traits of people you want to keep away?
how did you lose your optimism?
where are the places you don't fit?
who is in bed now with the love of your life?
when did your dreams turn to nightmares?
who is your least favorite family member?
what made you stop believing in surprises?
who damaged you the most?
where did you experience solitude?
in what year did you give up?

atoms and stories

he used to be jovial and calm,
but not anymore;
corpses do not laugh.
once this is over,
how many people would i have lost?
she said:

we're made out of atoms.
he is still somehow out there.

i told her we're made of stories.
he is still somehow in our memories.

poet's diet

whiskey and pain.

intermittence

every now and then, i feel a brutal stab.
the very food i eat, the very wind on my skin,
feel like long, stinging blades creeping through me.
when the city was hushed at the wee hours of the morning,
i could hear a menacing despair taking root in me

by the time i am able to tell myself the truth,
i'd better know how to breathe in the murk.

.

blurry

to the best of my understandingly shaky recollection,
the first time i committed suicide,
it went something like this.

sweet cake

i silently blew the candles out and wished for the courage
to finally grab a knife to cut my wrists and die.
happy birthday, may all your wishes come true,
they all said.

me:

i want everything to stop,
but i'm not sure about this... i'm afraid.

some wicked part of me:

keep going,
keep cutting.
it will be over soon.
just do it.
go,
cut,
do it!
it will all be over soon.
do it!
yes, yes, yes.

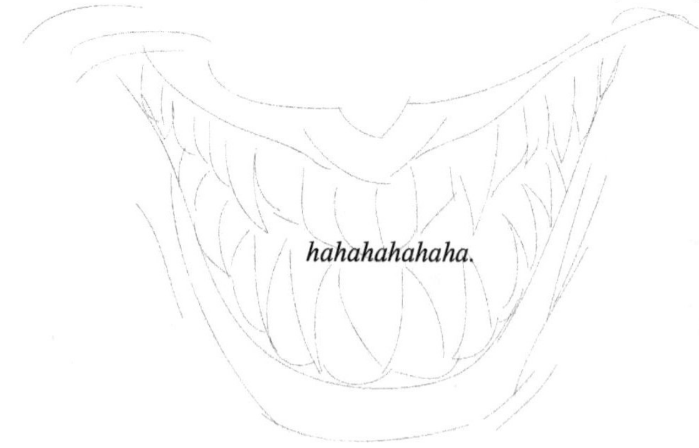

apartment anxiety

quietness reigns, and
i would hear the sound of the boiler,
of the water traveling through rusted pipes.
bedtime arrived; my alarm rang.
i would scribble on white paper
with black ink and blacker thoughts.
i would hear the silence of the night.
i would hear the voices of my ghosts yelling until sunrise.

red exorcism

a malevolent force
pushed the knife into
a clean wrist.

the bizarre sensation
is unforgettable.
the fortitude to slice the skin,
panic as the blood paints the scene—
a horrid synthesis.

i am not afraid to die,
but i'm terrified to forfeit my spirit,
letting my last thoughts
from my whole existence
be a bunch of nonsense.

at the doors of perpetual darkness,
my soul chose light.

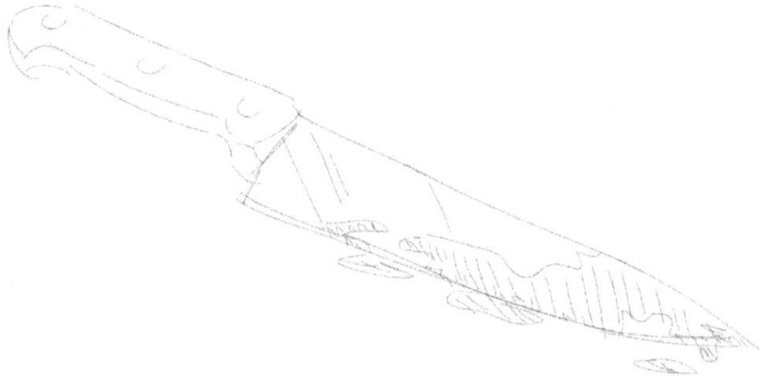

time prison

from time to time,
i write paragraphs
that throw me off,
and i can't recover.

from time to time,
i relive events
that dismember
my mental health.

from time to time,
words trap me
in a room where
woes betide me.

from time to time,
i escape in a couple of hours.
from time to time,
in a couple of years.

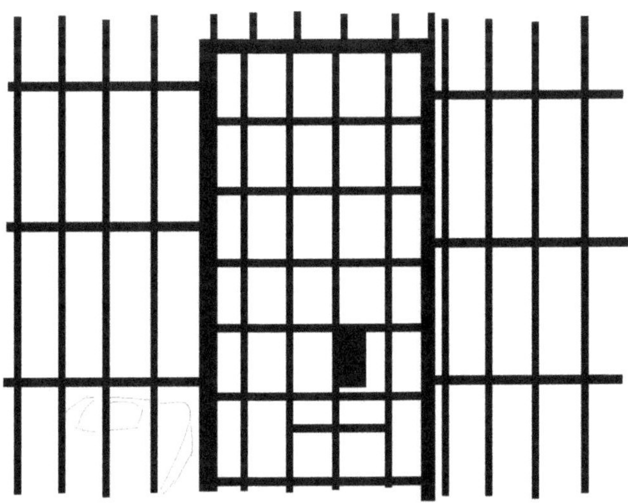

...

no one exists on purpose.
no one matters.
no one belongs anywhere.
nowhere matters.
nothing lasts.
everybody is going to die.

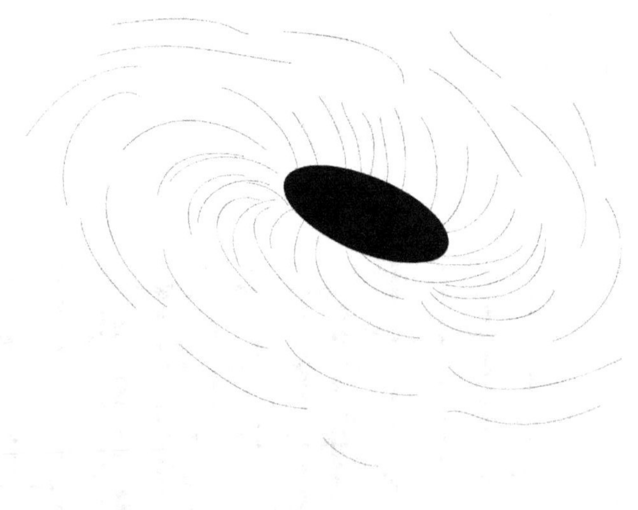

pause

slacking

i'm on my chair
      watching a pair of
schmucks
      on youtube
videos.

the first playlist
ends,
      then the twenty-third.

                  i'm bored
                      with
              writer's block.

              no one to tease,

nothing to scribble.
                  i'm stuck with you.

is this confusing?

              good.
          you're not the only one,
                      dumbass.

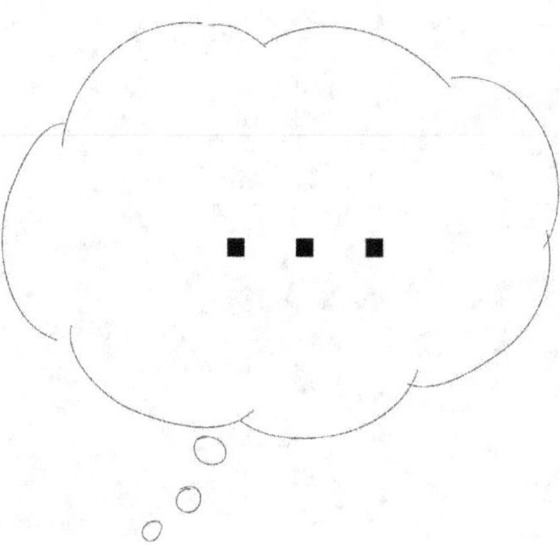

a brief story of eternity

Music in Prehistory, in the Ancient World, Egypt, Mesopotamia, Greece and Rome. Songs in traditional China, the Middle Ages, and in the early Catholic Church. Vocal austerity of the Gregorian Chant preceding Ars Nova and Polyphony. The Renaissance melodies in Italy, England, Germany, Spain and France. One early Flemish School, then the Baroque. Classicism against an Orchestra filled with new musical forms. A crescendo from the Manheim School expiring under the sparks of the Mediterranean classic plays. Pianos possessed by Romanticism, programmatic lullabies, the Lied, Nationalism and Romantic Symphonies. Russia, the group of five, Bohemia Smetana and Dvořák, Scandinavian influences too. Post-romanticism, Expressionism, Futurism. Consumerism, Pop, Socialist Realism and Impressionism in the 20th Century. Dodecaphonic compositions, Serialism and a Second Vienna School. Le Groupe des Six is so different from Electronic, Concrete, Jazz, and many variants. The cinema and influence of other new arts, Rock, Pop-rock, Fusion, Underground and Progressive. Techné and logos all over the XXI century. Numbers into sounds, theory to practice, musicians with singers, individuality and collectivity. Technology drying creativity, disenchantment and monotony. The role virtuoso is no longer conceived, machines produce tones impossible to humanely interpret, the machine uses the man. Rebellion, denial, diversity, freedom, difference, individuality. Distrust in tradition, rhythm, harmony and alienation. Songs that objectify the will and deepest secrets of mankind, sounds coming from the pleasure and virtue of enjoying, loving and hating. The analogy of the man and the melody, the tonic is stability, the dissonance is transgressive search. The dissonant man finds no rest and the man who only passes it on the tonic finds a stable monotonous life. Music translates the universal feelings ante rem into a reality in rem, its deeper message can't be reduced to language and words as it propounds a non-discursive nature: reveal and at the same time hide. And as it begins where language ends, music echoes the voice of another hereafter world naming the unnamable and communicating the non-communicable. Sounds and silences outside the limits of reason, an eloquence that can't be understood, only sensed. Can you sense it? The thousands of years, ancestors, wars, protests, romances, and religions in one single song. The soon to come eras, dreams, fantasies, tragedies and challenges in that piece of Eternity? Can you sense how touching the rules of music fundamentally alters the laws of everything? Since I sensed it, the world was no longer the same; since then, I hoped for our music not to stay the same.

once one loved something ...

> violin chords mold moods.
> clash of strings, vibes: smooth.
> major scale, tympanum tattoos.
> once found, easy to be fond of.
> if it's once adored,
> it becomes ubiquitous.

... one finds it everywhere

the need for ai

our technology nowadays is similar
to the ancient world wonders;
millions of pieces put together
with archaic methods
made with brute force and
thousands of slave-like workers.

how are you today?

happy
blessed
loved
sad
lovely
thankful
excited
in love
crazy
grateful
blissful
fantastic
silly
festive
wonderful
cool
amused
relaxed
positive
chill
hopeful
joyful
tired
motivated
proud
alone
thoughtful
sick
delighted
drained
emotional
confident
fresh
awesome
determined
exhausted

annoyed
glad
lucky
heartbroken
bored
sleepy
energized
hungry
professional
pained
peaceful
disappointed
optimistic
cold
cute
fabulous
great
sorry
super
worried
funny
bad
down
inspired
satisfied
pumped
calm
confused
goofy
missing
good
sarcastic
lonely
strong
concerned
special
depressed
jolly
curious
low

welcome
broken
beautiful
amazing
irritated
stressed
incomplete
hyper
mischievous
amazed
fed up
puzzled
furious
refreshed
accomplished
surprised
perplexed
frustrated
pretty
better
guilty
safe
free
lost
old
lazy
worse
horrible
comfortable
stupid
ashamed
terrible
asleep
well
alive
shy
rough
weird
human
hurt

awful
normal
warm
insecure
weak
kind
fine
dumb
nice
important
crappy
uncomfortable
worthless
ready
different
helpless
awkward
drunk
overwhelmed
hopeless
whole
miserable
mad
deep
yucky
nervous
blue
wanted
honored
light
hung-over
secure
naked
dirty
unimportant
mighty
scared
jealous
sore
unwanted

appreciated
full
busy
small
unloved
useless
qualified
blah
impatient
privileged
trapped
thirsty
nauseous
upset
offended
numb
perfect
challenged
threatened
relieved
stuck
strange
embarrassed
rested
smart
cheated
betrayed
anxious
aggravated
evil
ignored
regret
healthy
generous
rich
afraid
broke
invisible

most often i feel
"meh."

wittgenstein's game

i'm limited by language.
it is impossible for me to connect
with all of you to the same degree.

traveling through these pages,
you'll find messages in foreign tongues.
they are my meager attempt
to consider diversity.

i wish, despite the language barriers,
to touch similar souls to mine.

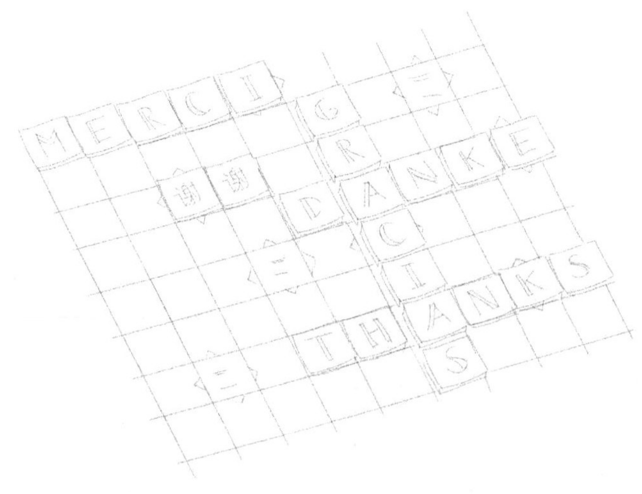

merci

demain, viendra l'orage, et le soir, et la nuit.
après-demain, les tonnerres, et la pluie, et les éclairs viendront.
aujourd'hui, le soleil brille jusqu'à ce que ton départ vienne.

seesöhne

Es wird mehr doch die Galaxis.
Je planmäßig wir vorgehen, desto leerer der Sinn.
Wir werden alle in der Stille sterben, zerfallen und verderben.

Zwischen Hölle und Firmament, die Existenz.
Die summe unseres Lebens sind die Sekunden,
in denen wir uns verloren in dem klang des Meeres Eloquenz.

谚语

近水知鱼性,近山识鸟音。

守得云开见月明。凡人不可貌相

海水不可斗量。

Aventureros

criaturas sensacionales, kilómetros de venas y arterias
que palpitan al unísono. tienen un fascinante talento
para vivir más de lo que sueñan, de hacer más de lo que dicen,
de creer más de lo que dudan y sentir más de lo que piensan.
se dirigen hacia las costas, hacia los bosques, hacia otros corazones.
nacen con una destreza inigualable para crear historias en el aburrimiento,
y se emocionan, ríen, miran, y aman con la misma intensidad de un incendio.
y así, escribir sobre ellas, que me lean, que mis letras las inspiren, y que su
suave y desnuda libertad me permita seguir vistiéndolas con mis palabras.

pluralism

the apparent multiplication of truths is bewildering at first glance;
promptly, you reckon it is one in many forms:
inclusion, tolerance, peace.
tilaka on forehead.
namaste.

calm of panglao

i hear people in here
talking about tarsiers,
scuba diving, waterfalls,
sunset yoga and motorbikes,
cave springs, rice fields, and chocolate hills.

         there's so much to discover.
         yet—i still need some more peace
         under the healing depths of this beautiful sea.

scuba diving

she placed in my mind the picture of diving
within the wrecks of the s.s. thistlegorm at the red sea.
places that show you how tiny you and your problems are…
explore, dream, discover.

bike ride 1:00 am

laugh, smile, cry, wonder, kiss, and get wild.
go ahead, enjoy the ride
with what you have, how you can,
with whomever you want.

sunset relaxation

yoga happens when you attend to your peace.
inhale the future, hold the present, exhale the past.

simple life

white on rice, green on grass, sheets on bed, eat, sleep, repeat.
isn't simple life tasty enough? i don't know…

free spirit

bohemian vibe:
    feet are dirty,
hair is messy,
    and eyes are wild.
rum for now.
    gypsy life.
soon it will be time to run fast.

azure confidences

5:00 in the morning,
music,
      dance,
            people,
                 sunrise,
                     and the ocean.

              the water was rubbing my drunken body.
                    i can't recall much,
       but my skin still recalls the salty sea secrets
            as if they were told yesterday,
and i still recall the ocean waves whispering to my skin.

schwarzbald haibun

i think of dawns, a cock's crow, breakfast resting on the grill.
thy abundant jade leaves paint the view from the balcony.
how many reality escapes dost thou facilitate?
perhaps i connect with thee and cut the wires of things outside thy realm.
again, i desire to take thee beyond the hut inside thy gut,
again, an improbable dream.
descend over daily activities, and from thy tranquility, lend peace to anxiety.

the thick mist conceals
cozy life with cedar scent
chop! chimney crackling.

wander

i'll never try to fit in; it is my uniqueness
that opens me to enjoy the aesthetics
of withdrawal.

breathe the entirety of those gawking moments
where we meet the limits of our language.

https://bit.ly/2021vida

did we feel the same?

adventurer's joy

the difference between an adventurer and a tourist relies on the irresistible
impulse to explore every situation until its very limits. amazing experiences do
not lay in foreign lands, one finds them in foreign souls.

i rejoice when my footprints become the judges of what i'm going to do.
i'm jubilant to travel and to be what i am right there and then.
i prefer being forced to trust strangers over the familiar comforts of home and
friends. i enjoy risking going too far and finding out how far my limits are.
it's my delight to be constantly off balance. i cherish being poor and owning
only air, sleep, dreams, the sea, the sand, the sky.

i am when my existence is reduced to either
a daring adventure or nothing at all.

inner party

you can travel everywhere,
escape from everyone,
and run away from everything.

but you can't elude your mistakes,
regrets, worries, and memories;
you can't run away from you.

it doesn't matter where you are
and with whom you are.
enjoy yourself! enjoy life!

himalaya haiku

a buddhist temple,
meditation dims the smell—
yuck! of yak butter.

i heard no people, no cars, zero subways, no cattle.
everything was hushed, and i realized that i was
at the world's quietest time. i was sitting at

the heart of silence

the one time that i sincerely prayed,

i prayed to no god, i do not believe in any. i prayed to have an honest conversation with myself, to participate fully in my inner reality with gratitude and serenity. humble and grounded, i prayed not to change an outcome, but for my mind to hear my soul's truest wishes, to slowly, steadily transform the nature of my actions and reactions.

the one time that i sincerely prayed,

i besought for an incredible journey towards nothingness.

truce

vhs tape

Fred sits at the end of a long day. He turns on his TV to relax and starts a monologue with the people on the screen. I observe carefully and pay attention to his words.

If I wanted to watch the same stuff I do in my job, I'd stay at work. The hell with monotony.
Again, these super-rich jerks with things I don't have, why do they like to rub it in my face?
This show again? I hate narcissistic people playing dumb. The hell with hedonism.

Fred continuously changes the channels complaining about everything on the screen.

Do I look like a person who would watch people pray during his free time?
Ha! Look at that comedy clown, c'mon people this joke doesn't even make me smile.
Ugh... this sport is so pointless. Wow, you moved the ball like no one and won. Yay!

What are you looking for Fred? I whisper to myself.

The news with agendas, reporting opinions and partial "facts." I digest none of those lies.
This motivational garbage is telling me that no randomness exists, give me a break.
I hoped for music, but it seems that only noise is played on these channels.

Everything seemed meaningless to Fred and so he shat all over the shows.

What's the point of documentaries? Awareness is not useful to me aside from complaining.
History reminds us to stop living in the past, yet we repeat many atrocious actions.
These makeover programs are trash. In two weeks, you'll return to your old pathetic self.

Fred's comments are the ones of an anguished man, what is he worried about?

Who the fuck finds love on TV? Stupid people selling what sells well.
Look at those pretending to be important. They sleep, eat, and defecate equally as me.
These guys are just teaching people how to be like them. What a bunch of hypocrites.

Fred's words went on, but in a snap of time, he started to sound less petty and more serious.

Trying hard to mask misery gives birth to the underworlds that we hide. Misery dwells in negation and habitats in "meaning." People shine with the dark brightness of unshared suffering. They are living proof of the first law of human thermodynamics:
<u>Misery is neither created nor destroyed; it is only transformed</u>.

I hear the bells of the clock, bedtime arrives, and I've had enough of Fred's show.
So, I stand up, approach my TV and take the tape out of the VHS. One could read the title of the record written in Greek. Fred's message is more incisive than I expected.
I get you, pal, we are all together in this Sisyphus myth of absurdity.

late days of covid-19

95,479,062 reported cases,
over two million of corpses,
people's irresponsibility,
infinite truths exposed,
families destroyed,
anxiety, and confinement prolonged,
a clutch of clutch vaccines
approaches, and we clutch
to the hope of clutching back to the life
we once complained about very much.

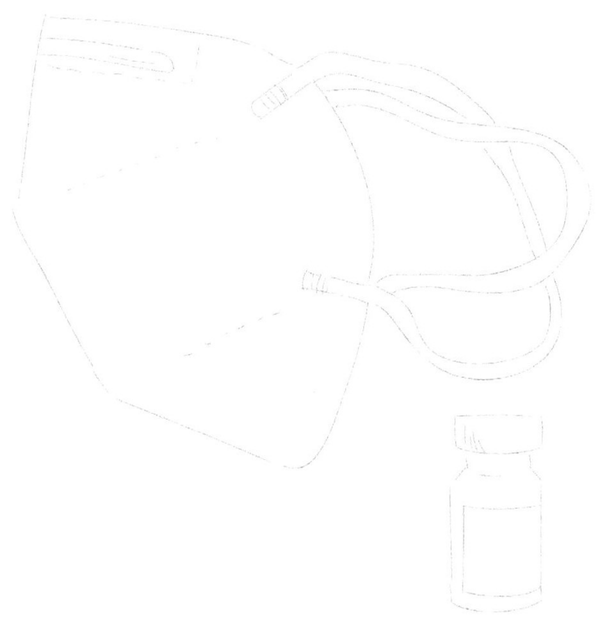

need to fill

it's not the substance that makes you an addict.
it's the need to escape reality, to shut it down.
touch rock bottom. there you'll find the first stone to rebuild.
you are worth it.

where are the answers?

doubts shot at him,
like balls from a football launcher,
one after another,
without a care or concern about where they landed.
but he didn't know how to play ball; he hadn't played sports his whole life.

lost

no one advised me on how to live.
all i wanted was to run as far as possible
away from the places everyone else walked towards.
how easy it is for people that already have a guide in their life.
i guess i'll just have to look for one in places i don't expect.

i'm looking for a mentor or at least a soul to resonate with.

silver lining

three years ago, someone threw a rope and shouted:

yo! do you want to get out from that dark pit?

well, you got a long way to climb.

unpunctuality

there are those moments that keep you in the past.
those moments came delayed, but echoed precisely.
a warning comes when everything feels so real, but nothing normal.
the hit arrives when you understand that life tarries with the answers
and by the time you get them, all of the questions will have already changed.

i call this the fundamental asynchronous nature of life.

masks off

why hide the scars, to keep pretending? show what is deeply buried in pain.

be beautiful, not like in the magazines, but just as you are, for what sparkles in your eyes when you talk about something you love, beautiful for your ability to make people smile even when you are broken with sorrow.

no, don't be beautiful for something as temporary as looks; be beautiful for what is deep inside in you.

preach about the power of trying because it's fine to fail, preach about generosity to battle selfishness.

preach about joy because you know hell; preach wishes for all that lost their hope; preach for what is to be broken and in seek of nothingness, and i'll preach for gratitude because i am grateful for all of it.

différance

<table>
<tr><td>

i am joy

i am a blessing

i have secrets

every day i fight the sadness

caused by madness

we are total opposites

i am humble

people admire me for my work

i have a sidekick

without madness

i am nothing!

</td><td>

i am madness

i am a curse

i have secrets

everyday i injure hopes

which are healed by joy

we are total opposites

i crave attention

people fear me for my work

i have an accomplice

without joy

i am nothing!

</td></tr>
</table>

opposites waltz

light doesn't avoid darkness. on the contrary,
their incessant dance unveils the magic
of fireworks, auroras, and skylines.
share your light when someone shows darkness.

one day

sometimes i wish for only one more day to live,
and so, recover these twenty-seven years lost,
vomit the totality of my thoughts, love my dearest ones,
empty me from the stupidity of quotidian life,
and fill me with a woman whose smile is worth gambling my own life.
sometimes i'd wish for her to tell me that there is no tomorrow,
and so, i could stop the bullshit, toast in bed with our bodies,
bite her skin until i undress her soul, get drunk with looks,
laugh from tragedies, and die on the beach in a hammock.

failed suicide

i quit guitar lessons and swimming.
i quit competitions and trainings.
i quit relationships and university.
i quit business and writing.
i tried to quit life once and…

i've never quit anything since then.

fierce

experiencing a tragedy is not brave, but returning to the tragedy to conquer, scared and still, is the product of a brave irrationality that urges to glare at the gaze of fear and shout: "i'm here, i'm not moving" while the rational and biological voice says: "let's run, let's flee to safety."

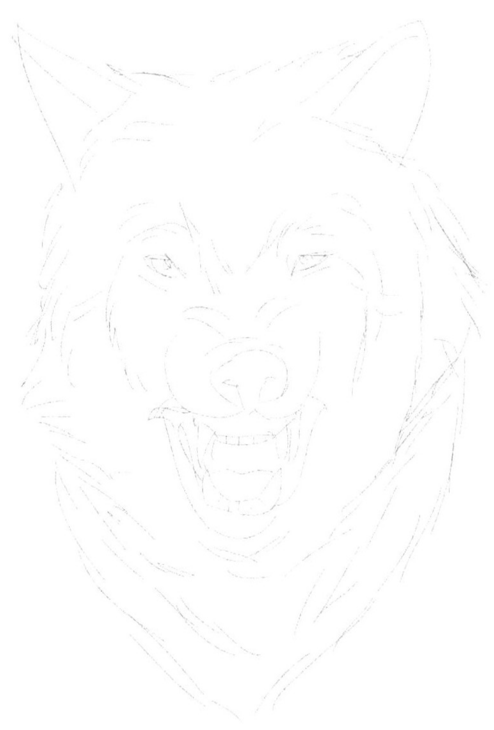

just once

i don't often recall the things
that i easily got.

a prize without a fight
hinders my warrior pride.

when i dream of something,
i'm prepared to try twice or thrice.

in reality, it finally comes
after the hundredth time.

fighting for my goals
fills me with reinvigorating strength.

yet, it would be nice if something
came easy now and again.

winds color blue

there i was, crossing borders by sea
and journeying deep in my thoughts.

while sailing, a change of winds means a change of course.
original plans change, we hit shores sooner than expected.

life has that kind of magic.

unchained

there's no going back, as there is nothing to go back to.

memo to my present self

tired of the grit of sleepless nights?
drained by frustration, and tantrums?
c'mon your tenacity isn't even halfway!
you'll turn many dreams to memories,
even some you could never imagine.

you'll learn to let go.
embrace the things yet to come.
stop until you get everything
we've dreamed of.
you owe it to all of us,
to every version of you.

guide to be absurd & crazy

step 1:
pursue your dreams.
step 2:
discover that your existence is absurd
and your goals meaningless.
step 3:
try harder.

gentleness

during one warm dawn in march,
i said to myself that
i wouldn't want to become
similar to the bullies i hate.
since then, and after witnessing,
incarnating amiability,
i embraced a strict
no aggression policy.

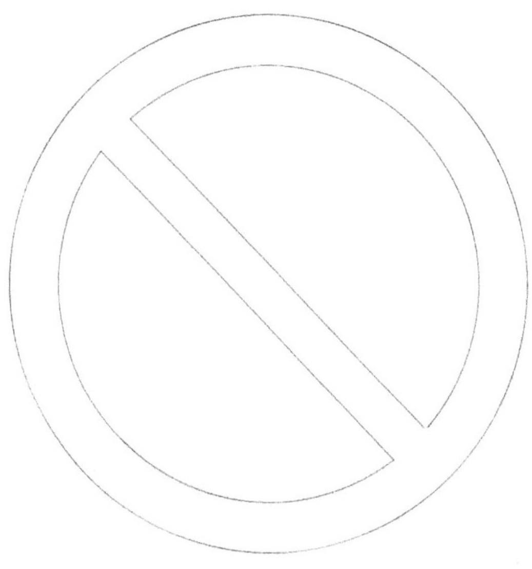

my advice

i'm as confused as all of you.
i've just made a habit out of it.
i've come to appreciate and want confusion;
it is a stimulating promise of a treasure.

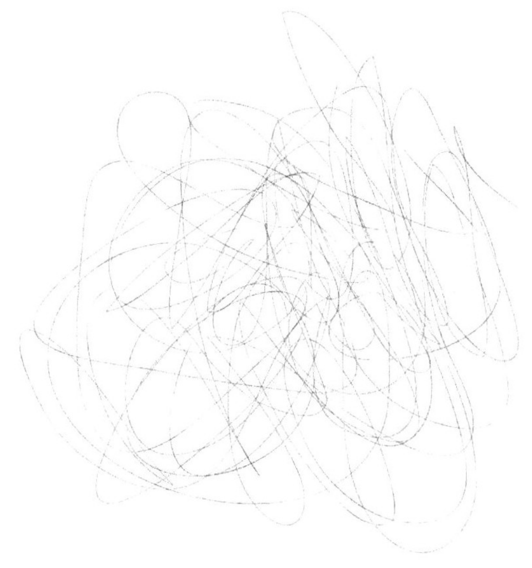

optimist nihilist

i read the pessimism in my head; i mean, i believe practically in nothing,
yet i possess an optimistic heart that makes me do shit nonstop.
in this bipolarity, i swung the last lustrum,
and like the things that make no sense, life went on.

pain billionaire

i crave pain; it is my every night's dream;
i passionately search for vast amounts.
imagine the things i wouldn't do with such wealth.
the bad news i wouldn't cry about,
the attacks i wouldn't feel,
the betrayals i wouldn't resent.
i'd like to be a pain billionaire:
grains of sand do not alter a desert.

until

until your skin confesses to your soul that it dies slowly of not bathing in the ocean, you will not know what it is to really feel the sea.

until you cry and laugh with a book, you will not have truly read.

until you feel a change within you, without being able to take your eyes off the screen, you will not have seen good cinema.

until your body loses control and your smile bursts by listening to wordless melodies, you will not have heard music.

until you close your eyes and notice how the magic takes over every corner of your body until it faints, you will not have danced.

until you break your lip with a punch and taste your own blood, you will not have fought.

until you cum with that person for whom you would gamble your own life, you will not have fucked.

until the frenulum of your tongue hurts the next day, you will not have eaten a pussy.

until you feel that there is a piece of you that is no longer yours, you will not have loved.

until you are short of breath, until the seconds are not millennia, you will not have a clue what it is to miss.

until you understand that pride is the only language that does not exist among friends, you will not know what friendship is.

until you feed your vitality, you will not know what the hell it is to feel.

make it rain

i spend words, i spend pages, i spend stories, i spend looks, i spend songs,
i spend walks, i spend my malnourished income, i spend wishes, i spend
caresses, i spend kisses, i spend sex and semen, tears and heartbeats, i spend
dinners and brunches, i spend whispers, drops of sweat and screams of
happiness, i spend silences, i spend evenings, i spend good wine and countless
bottles of beer, i spend conversations until the early morning, i spend a bunch
of gut, i spend defects, a lot of them, i spend moments with my friends,
i spend days and years. what was once reserved for rare moments is now a
mindset. i plan to spend it all and leave nothing for death.

risky excitement

something is missing.
every aspect seems under control.
the blitz of adrenaline is not enough.
quicker, harder, stormier
until the thrill of danger
overcomes the fear of death.

lush

why do you enjoy the pain?
why be vulnerable to danger?
why are you an addict to that rush?
because from time to time, dancing with death lets you take life to bed.

dear friend

She badgers me to observe others, and I ponder.
The majority of people avoid mentioning her; they preach that she brings agony,
fear, and pain to our loved ones, that she gifts denial, anger, bargaining,
depression, and acceptance to oneself. After meditations, only uncertainty
remains.

She pesters me to doubt antonyms, and I ponder.
Light versus dark—the latter isn't the lack of the former—black, white, hot, cold,
good, evil, day, and night. Absence brings void, where something cannot be
conceived from nothing. Ignore contraries, everything is one same thing observed
through diverse spectacles.

She nags me to know her, and I ponder.
Where on earth are the individuals who ended a friendship with her? They're to
be found in another realm perhaps. Talking about an arrival seems like nonsense;
my plan is to flirt with my friend until all the secrets are flashed with an
enlightening farewell.

She urges me to appreciate her, and I ponder.
Statues, books, and research are made in the name of my friend. Procreation
makes sense because of her. She's a time thief—without her, we'd have zero to
think and naught to do. We'd eventually have thought and done everything. We'd
have a lot to see, but infinite years to see it.

She compels me to perceive my body, and I ponder.
My flawless homeostasis resists the attrition of the world, and my equilibrium
weakens until its energy surrenders to the entropy of the macrocosm. Chaos and
disorder will ultimately claim their place in my perfectly ordered anatomy.

She is a difficult friend to deal with, and I ponder.
She has held my hand since the day of my birth. She gives meaning to my actions
by giving me the opportunity to embrace the ephemerality of human life. She
reminds me of the darkness, a place I was before being born and my destination
once she is gone.

twenty-seven years of dancing together, and I ponder.
Oh, my sweetest, don't go just yet; without you I can't keep dying. Let me die
over low fire until I feel satisfied. Please hear my request: allow me to walk with
you many more days, my dearest friend, *Death*.

conversations

i fancy individuals with blurred recall. who talk with emotions from a crooked heart; ugh, i hate small talk. i vamoose inside chats about sins and mistakes too expensive to misspend on vain regrets.

underappreciated lies,

are powerful in our lives;
we condemn them and praise the truth,
but we overlook their importance.

these are the lies we tell to ourselves—
lies we know are false, but we disguise as truths.
lies we tell to avoid conflict.
lies we work so hard to transform into facts.

i trust lies because they reveal more from you than the truth.
in a single lie you reveal what is intimate,
you protect your limits and insecurities.
lie to me please, so i can dive deep into your fears.

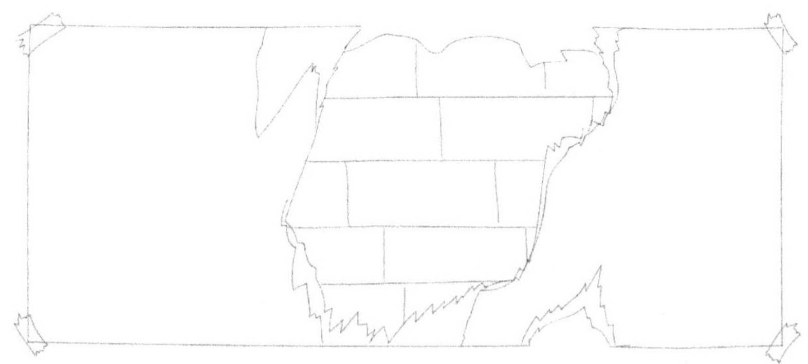

perennial doubts

that night, they discussed until the sunrise,
trying to agree on several perennial questions.

do we live in an indifferent universe?
or does the universe take care of us?
what or who orders and decrees our destiny?

what is the physical nature made of?
and according to what principles does it operate?

what is a human?

is society static or dynamic?
changing or immutable?
machine or organism?
what is more real, the society or the individual?

what is the meaning of the past?
do we stick to it?
or forget about it?
does history advance towards something?
does it have a goal?
god's or human's will?

and like people before them,
they ended up with more doubts than answers,
unable to agree on concepts beyond them:
god, nature, humanity, society and history.

whale shark

> he doesn't contemplate yesterday and today,
> swims from one side to the other, eats, rests,
> digests, and swims again. day by day, night after night,
> he's tied with a short distance to his joy and far from pique.
> i envy his happiness, his tranquility—
> no weariness, no pain,
> zero melancholy.

i'm too human

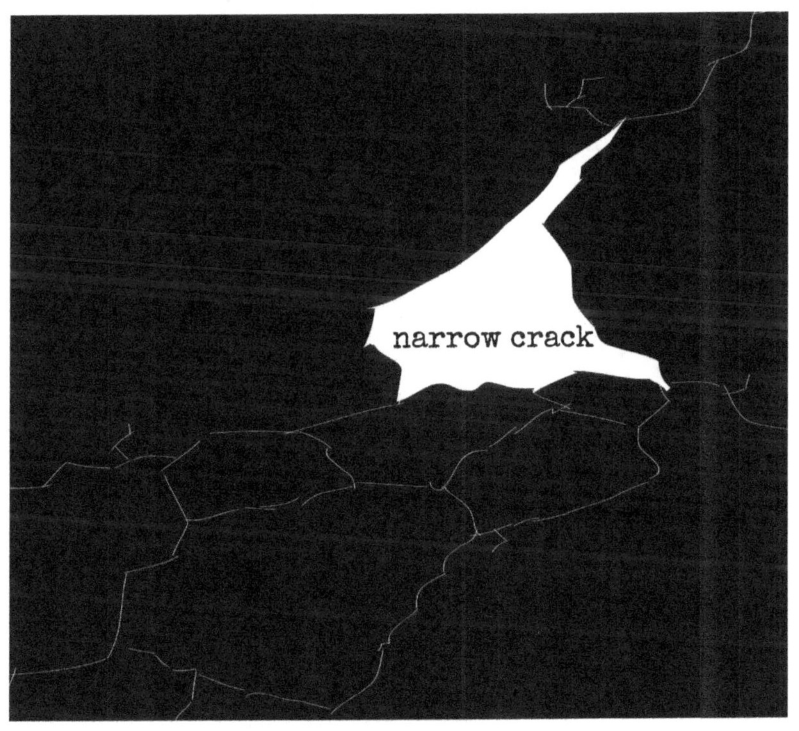# narrow crack

i figured out how to stay alive with relative ease,
but to find something to live for, well,
that's perhaps a much more bewildering complication:
how do i expand an ephemeral crack between two dark eternities?

room to improve

a person is what he is and his circumstances.
he is what is lost and what remains.
in a way, we are and aren't at the same time.

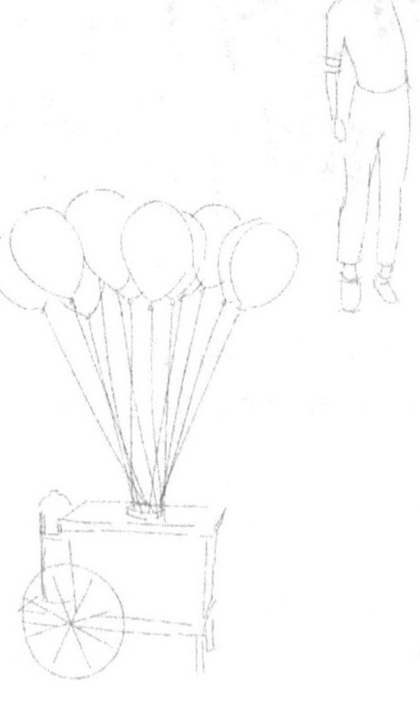

minimalist feng shui remodel

the home interior is

full of clutter, expensive objects; it's baroque with no natural light.

examine the possessions piece by piece.

ask: <u>does this object still bring elation to my heart?</u>

remove noise from a palace of peace.

throw the result of constant hoarding.

get rid of redundant stuff.

be left with a sanctuary

of powerful serenity.

sources of slavery

one of the toughest lessons is being free—
free from guilt, anger, love, loss, happiness, or betrayal.
freedom isn't easy.
we fight to hold on,
but it's harder to let go of an unstoppable source of emotions.
nothing external can govern you internally.
understand this and be free.

nature is a paramour

once the campfire was cold coal and the laughs just snores,
i sat on the sand to watch the stars.
the silence, though, had an earthly presence that seduced my senses.
my mind got lost listening to a superb melody of tranquility.
i was submerged in a delusion; in it, nature incarnated in a woman, and i had
an unsatiable lust for her. the desire to relive everything was so strong that
it took me to stop thinking about it fourteen days and 300 nights.

impression, sourire

Blues and oranges,
brisk sun, hazy sky,
subtle warmth, cool winds;
bold vibration in a motionless scene.
Evanescent morning,
burning glow etching the water;
Indecipherable scenery
conveying an effect of infinity.
Clouds in spring,
harbor and docks,
wrinkled lips,
laxity of thoughts.
Mild freckles,
spontaneous chuckles,
fertile complexion,
cold gaze and auburn hair.
Blazing color
of an eerie feeling of trust,
blended shades
in a pair of coffee filled eyes.
Brushes of dappled daylight
rendered all into impressionistic art
of beige, russets and tan tones;
her body is the endless sea,
her voice, the kiss of wind,
her hair is the waves and tides,
her walk, the quake of land;
a landscape passes by,
and my Kuru laughter starts.
Alas, it is gone, but
to me, is to watch
Claude's Soleil Levant
every time I remember her smile.

kryptonite

by that age, i knew how to react to any danger,
but she attacked with her most powerful weapon.
she attacked me with her happiness,
and i didn't know what to do.

porcelain

i imagine us sharing tea, looking inwards and popping the big questions.
getting older by the minute, wiser by the words.
great tea and advice come from age.

sense of irony

we made a habit of cracking jokes
about anyone and anything,
and laughed and laughed.
our tummies hurt from mirth.
sadness and tragedy became comedies
we laughed at from the front row.

hakuna matata

an accelerating rise of energy,
not from confusion, but from a pure impulse.
releasing heart and soul to ignore time and place.
heat rises intensely and wildly.
the pile of secular problems, hesitation, panic, and fear
burns to nothing.
all foreign sensation dims and fades.
from a state of deeper instinct,
worries run away.

saharan

i had been on a long quest
to find a place like this,
an appropriate place to meditate,
deserted and calm.

> i sat before the dawn
> on a sea of red dust,
> investigating the sources
> of my anxiety.

my mind ran out of
plausible explanations,
and i kept it blank
suddenly.

> my inexperienced spirit
> suspected to have found
> what i desperately needed,
> quietness and isolation

is this how i achieve inner peace?
i speculated, and then, a heightened revelation began.

i commenced to sense the wind wafting my jillaba, the sunrays gently burning my skin, every grain of sand landing on my face, the swing of the rachises, the grunts of the camels, the scent of my body, the warm temperature, the moisture in the air, the clouds moseying along the heavens. in my silence, i heard nature's orchestra; in my stillness, i saw nature's incessant movement; in my tranquility, i found nature's chaos.

my concept of inner peace evolved; mine does not come from stopping the war in my mind, nor halting any noise from the outside, nor slowing down. as in nature, my harmony is shown on the surface as the result of trillions and trillions of fast uninterrupted processes. people, plants, animals, microorganisms, atoms, memories, doubts, desires, ideas, tragedies, and universal forces expanding into disarray.

i'm part of this fundamental disorder, too.
fighting against it, fighting against myself
will only bring me anxiety.
synchronizing my spirit with chaos
was what i needed to reach
immutable tranquility, vibrant calm, and a relentless state of mind.

unison

i'm free-spirited, but not detached from the world.
flexible, but not submissive.
firm, but not unchanging.
passionate, but not obsessed.

a fire with no smoke,
one warm sun,
no burns,
unconditional love.

shame forgotten,
anger controlled,

educated emotions
on a symbiosis
of brain and heart.

i find virtue by living,
avoiding ignorance
by indoctrination.

shy to share

i have a titan of a dream,
which is too colossal to mention.
my resilience pushes me to climb it
even when i know it will take me
ten lifetimes to merely reach its knee.

where's the line between goals and fantasy?

memo to my future self

after long, crazy years, the fatigue is no more.
you finally start building the greatest of your dreams.
yes, that one you keep to yourself.
you have not even the most remote clue of how to achieve it,
but you commit to a lifetime to reach it.
no one regrets being brave.

blueprints

your plans are subject to the ruthless scrutiny of chaos,
but don't close yourself to possibilities.
take leaps of dreams and imagination.
the excitement alone is worth it.

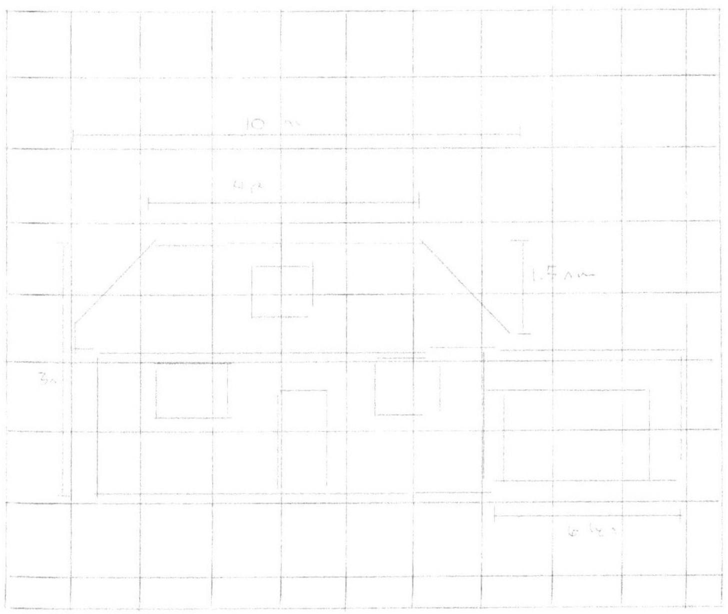

$$X_{n+1} = rX_n(1 - X_n)$$

small decisions,
bigger consequences—
somehow the short life of one
will give us a lasting survival to all.

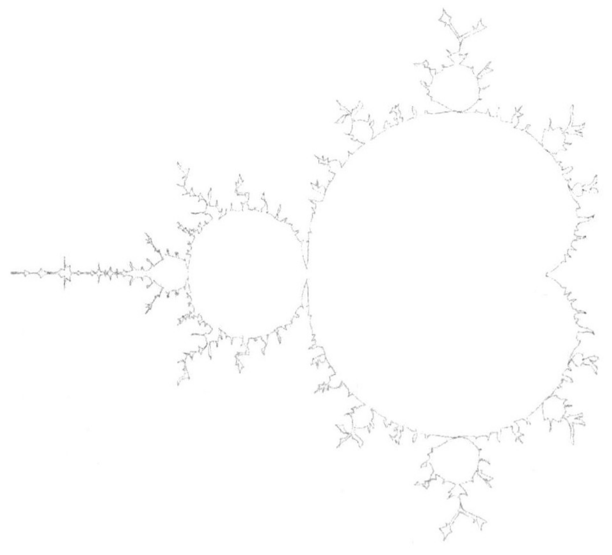

reasons to write:

to get the godlike feeling
of creating a galaxy with my rules.

to impersonate a scientist
contributing to the history of the human soul.

or is it to ease the craziness feasting on my entrails?

perhaps i write, simply, to end up
penniless in paris.

in the mind of a nihilist

we are all marching to darkness. when one closes the eyes and tries to remember the moments before birth, one is only encountered with the darkness that awaits. we block any resemblance of our inevitable despair, fed with distractions to please ego, vanity, contempt, and comfort. but as absurd as it sounds on many levels, we've got to embrace and smile at despair, make deference to darkness, and ring the knell of our deepest fears while we imperatively find a personal ontological answer to the question:

why do i do the things i do?

and in the face of the void, remember:

i'm not much, but i'm all i have!

amor fati

deconstruct common life

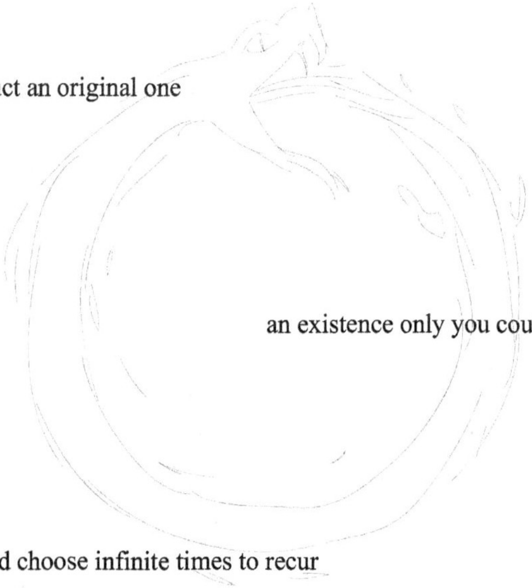

construct an original one

an existence only you could experience

one you would choose infinite times to recur

to remain in an eternal return.

eudaimonia

the older we are, the closer we are to life; we know it better
and are more connected to it. thus, the moment we have less time in it,
the more of life we have.

it is only at the end of life that we can say if we were happy or not,
if we were loved or not, if we were good or not.
in the last nanoseconds of our existence, we know it all.

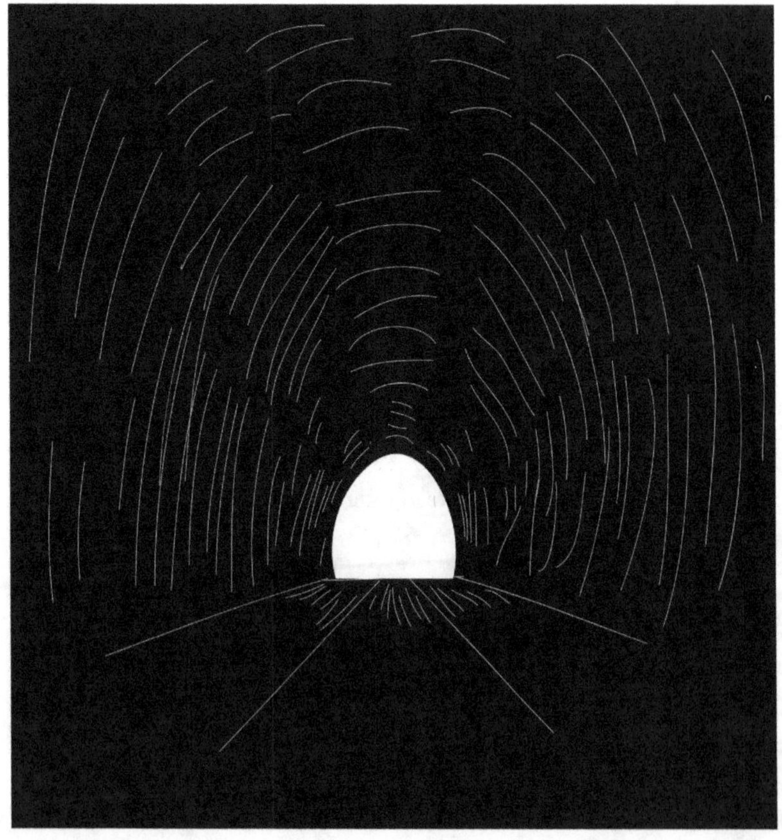

popper's falsificationism

i think the progress of our species doesn't rest
on the chase of what might be correct,
but by having an absolute certainty of what is not.
we will get, through an asymptotic movement, closer to our truth.

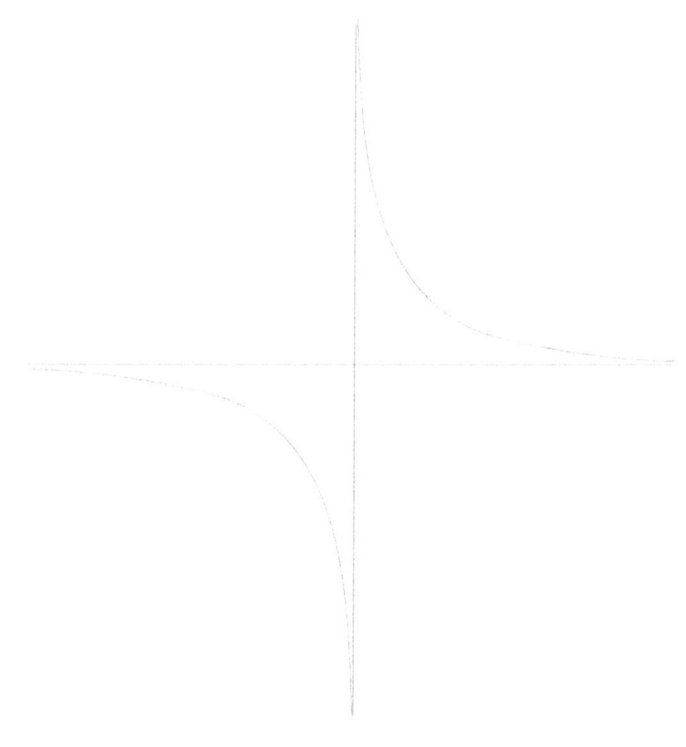

stoic duty

the way i see it,
the ultimate goal of our work should be giving our species
more time to survive
the longer we exist, the more chances we have to disprove our fake truths.

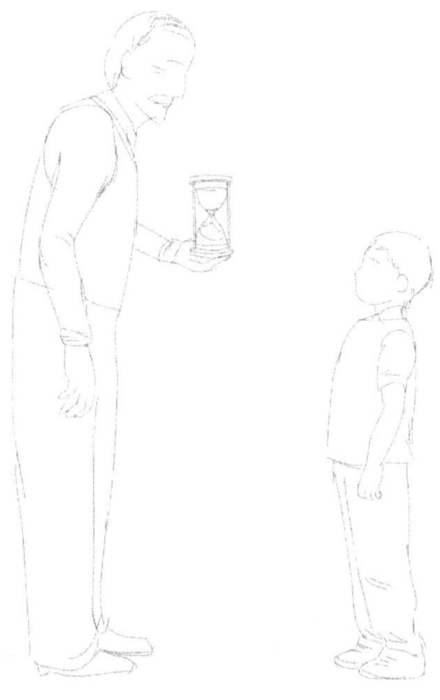

your life

i can't understand
people preferring
riches over life,
money over health,
putrefaction over nature.

i, as an individual, will live 70 years,
the milky way 4 billion,
our sun 9 billion,
planet earth 10^{25} years.

but for how long will our successors last?
i can only do futile work now
to inspire generations to come.
my life's purpose is to aid people,
my life is yours, too.

humanity's survival

i no longer live a life you would recognize, i no longer consider myself as an individual, which for a leader is a required mindset; i chose instead to submerge myself in a community of humanity.
i fused with a body that shares a common history, common values, and a common memory, the price of which is the surrender of oneself.

common martyr

"our resilience didn't take too much to collapse. our foe was merciless, decisive. but they weren't nimble enough. for you had already bequeathed the baton. and because of you, we found hope, uncovered its mysteries, squashed our adversary's purposefulness. our victory —your victory— was so nigh ... i yearn for a reality in which you could have survived enough to witness it. but you appertain to this soil. your body, your clothes— all burned and turned to ashes. everything was gone, except your courage. that, you handed out to us. and with it, we could reassemble."

-to everyone who died so that we might survive.

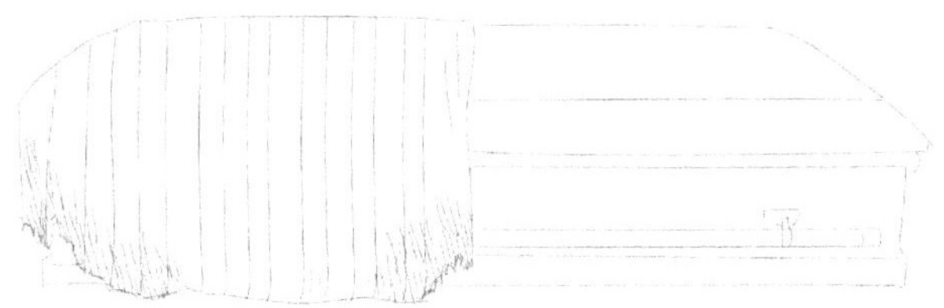

cigarette thoughts: life burns like tobacco

i am the aggregate of everything preceding me.
i'm a product of all i have perpetrated,
of everything that has befallen me.
i am all the lives whose existence was altered by mine.
i am every consequence that occurs after i'm gone,
which would not have become if i had not happened.
i risk my absence to affirm my presence.

my nihilism

i beheld that longcase clock; its mesmerizing swing evinced an epiphany of sorts. this path mimics a pendulum swiftly swaying between bliss and the dark. my soul gluts from delights, then with a sharp knife, i unhurriedly eviscerate my gut. it is a fine addiction stronger than morphine, being empty and hollow just to grasp the beginning of a new, thrilling, breathtaking sprint towards nothingness.

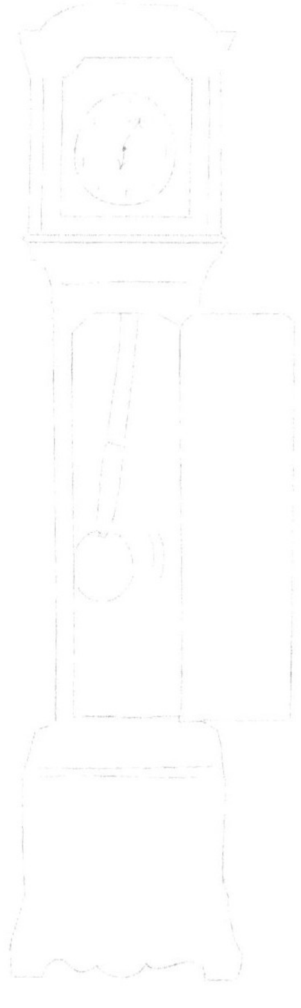

to you

my dearest,

carry me throughout your entire life as a sign of better things ahead.
carry me throughout moments of strength.
carry me throughout victories.
carry me throughout your greatest decisions.
carry me throughout each big lesson you learn.
carry me throughout smiles.
carry me throughout your steps.
carry me along, and i'll carry you through.

sincerely,
hope.

centaurea cyanus

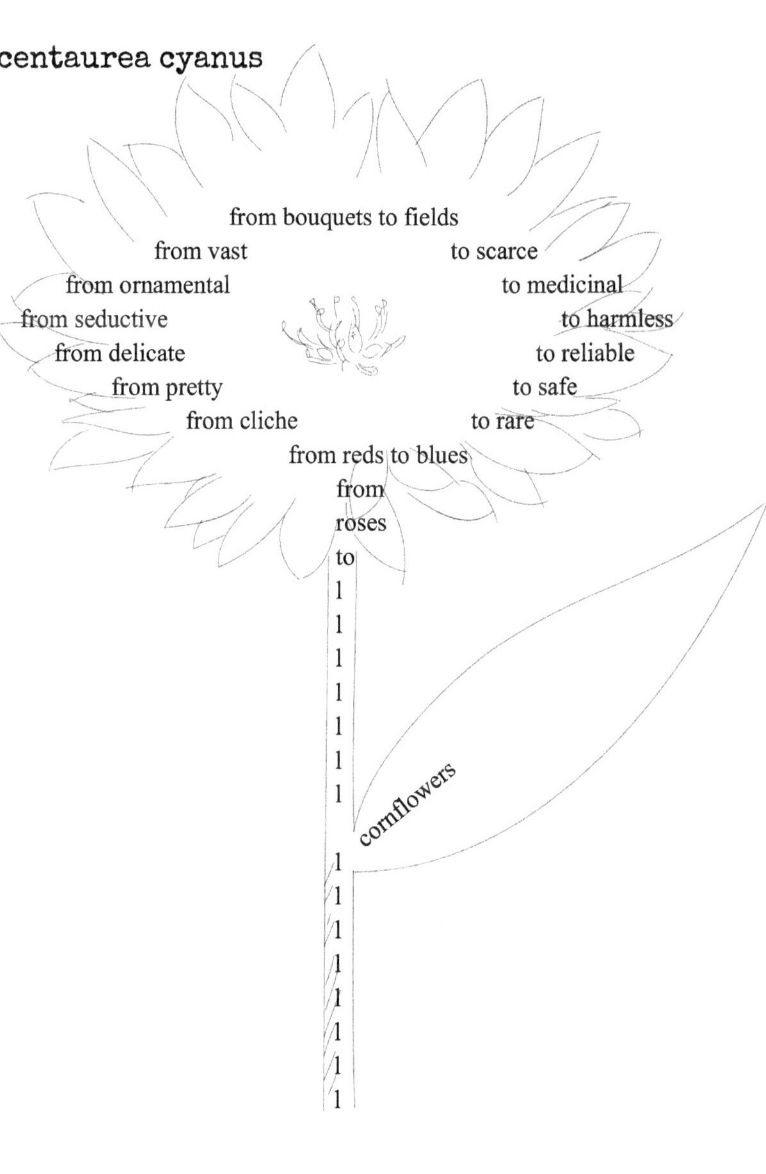

bookworm's food

how many books have been written?
how many are forgotten?

with the vast number of books published,
i do not expect my words to be massively read,
nor making a living from them.

i imagine, in the distant future,
a bookworm of sorts would find me
during an expedition to the forgotten shelves of an old library.

i envision my work resonating with a foreign mind centuries from now.
thus, securing through intermittent, lasting, rare events
my place in human posterity.
this book's only pretension is to be one serving of bookworm's food.

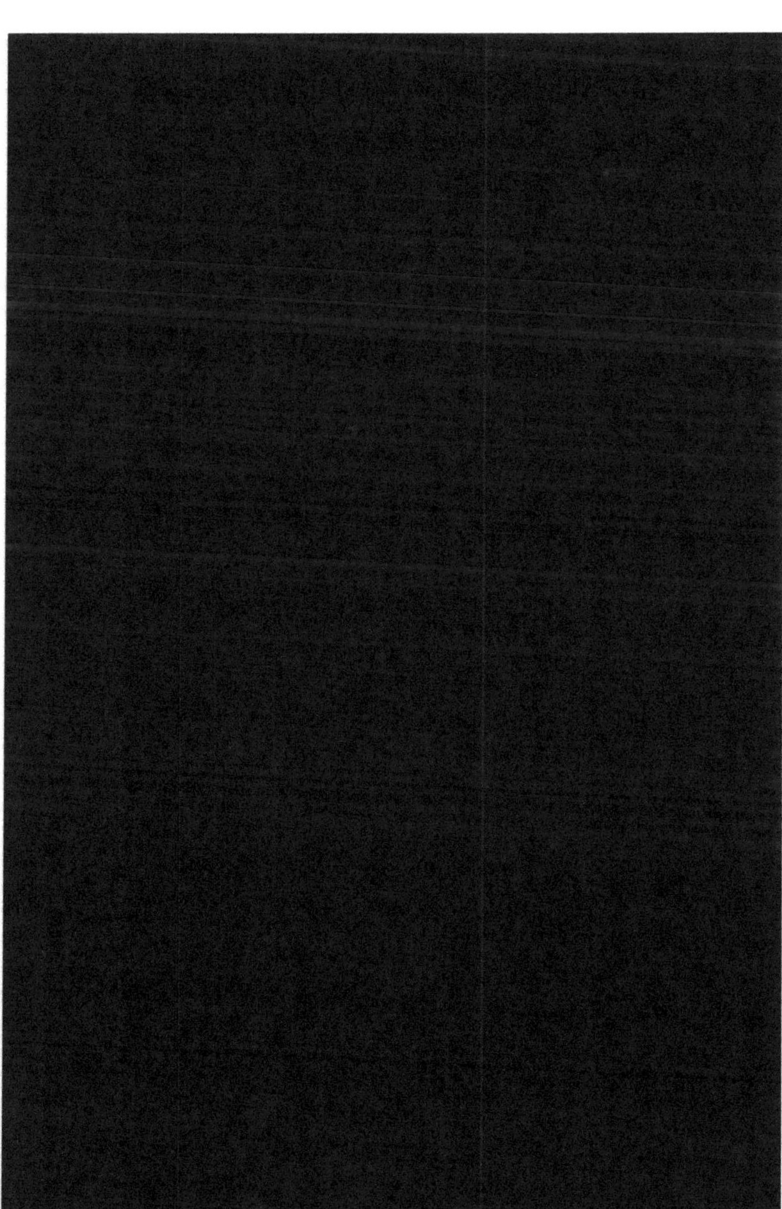

you have finished this story. with my voice in your thoughts.

thank you. for enduring the journey. for being empathetic with the most intricate part of me. smile, relax, you must be tired. let me praise your mind. your eyes. they must be wanting of something rewarding. i am sending all my compliments. you've helped me gain clarity. i would be quiet and hiding myself if it were not for you. do you have any idea how much of a blessing you are? i am immensely thankful. receive this token to remember that i'll be with you as long as i exist. let me repeat. you are not alone as long as i breathe. i am sending this token to your mind. may it always remain strong. may it expand, and may you always practice compassion. may our paths cross. may we love everything the universe has for us. may we always stay genuine, brave, our hearts prepared for the world.

- a token of my appreciation

aaron vergara moreno is a digital project manager born in mexico starting his journey as an experimental poet. throughout his work he addresses themes of resilience, loss, love, and philosophy. he shares his writing with his readers as a means to create an empathetic connection for acceptance, and grounded courage. his creative direction fosters self-contemplation with refreshing writing. when he is not writing, he travels to connect with the sentiments of other cultures, as well as engage daily in business ventures within the digital industry.

you can find more of his work at:

www.instagram.com/aaron.vergara

www.linkedin.com/in/aaronvergara

- about the author

www.ingramcontent.com/pod-product-compliance
Lightning Source LLC
Chambersburg PA
CBHW071500140726
47997CB00005B/1797